Gàir

The Harp's Cry

Colm Ó Baoill

Born in the City of Armagh in 1938 and educated there and at Queen's University, Belfast.

Assistant Lecturer in Celtic at Queen's 1962 and Lecturer in Celtic at Aberdeen University 1966.

Married Frances 1968, and they now have three daughters.

Edited the Gaelic poems of *Sìleas na Ceapaich* (c.1660–c.1729), published as *Bàrdachd Shìlis na Ceapaich* by the Scottish Gaelic Texts Society in 1972.

Edited a collection of 17th–18th-century Maclean poetry, published as *Eachann Bacach and other Maclean poets* by the SGTS in 1979.

Reader in Celtic at Aberdeen University 1992.

Meg Bateman

Was born in Edinburgh in 1959 and educated there. She learnt Gaelic as an adult, in South Uist and at Aberdeen University where she did a degree in Gaelic Studies and a doctorate on medieval Gaelic religious poetry. After graduating she taught Gaelic in Edinburgh to various groups while gaining some renown as a translator and poet in the language. In 1991 she returned as a lecturer to Aberdeen. Her poems have appeared in her collection, *Orain Ghaoil*, (Dublin 1990) and in the bilingual anthology, *An Aghaidh na Sìorraidheachd*, (Edinburgh 1991).

Gàir nan Clàrsach
The Harps' Cry

Edited by

COLM Ó BAOILL

Translated by

MEG BATEMAN

Birlinn

© Colm Ó Baoill and Meg Bateman 1994

Published by Birlinn Ltd
13 Roseneath Street
Edinburgh

Typeset in Monotype Plantin
by ROM-Data, Falmouth
and printed in Finland by
Werner Soderstrom OY

A CIP record for this book is
available from the British Library

ISBN 0 874744 13 0

Chuidich Comhairle nan Leabhraichean am foillsichear
le cosgaisean an leabhair seo

Contents

Preface   ix

Introduction   1

Translator's Note   41

Notes on the Tunes   45

I *Iomair thusa, Choinnich cridhe* (?1600)   48

II *A mhic Iain mhic Sheumais* (1601)   50

III MacGriogair à Ruaro (c. 1605)   54
Tha mulad, tha mulad

IV Ailean Dubh à Lòchaidh (1603)   58
'S toigh leam Ailean Dubh à Lòchaidh

V An spaidearachd Bharrach (?c. 1620)   58
A Dhia, is gaolach lium an gille

VI *Thugar maighdeann a' chùil bhuidhe* (?1611)   62

VII Do Ruaidhri Mòr, Mac Leòid (?1613)   64
Sé hoidhche dhamhsa san Dún
– Niall Mór Mac Muireadhaigh

VIII Tàladh Dhòmhnaill Ghuirm (?1617)   66
Ar liom gura h-ì a' ghrian tha ag èirigh

IX Saighdean Ghlinn Lìobhainn (?c. 1620)   68
A mhic an fhir ruaidh

X Cumha do Niall Og (?c. 1625)   74
Gur e mis tha air mo chùradh
– Mòr NicPhàidein

XI Air bàs mhic Mhic Coinnich (?1629)   76
Treun am Mac a thug ar leòn
– Donnchadh MacRaoiridh

XII Rainn do rinneadh leis na shean aois (c. 1630)   78
Fada ta mis an dèidh chàich
– Donnchadh MacRaoiridh

XIII Ceithir rainn do rinneadh leis an là a d'eug se   82
    (c. 1630)
Beir mise leat, a Mhic Dè
– Donnchadh MacRaoiridh

XIV Air leabaidh a bhàis (c. 1630)   84
Thàinig fàth bròin air ar cridhe
– Donnchadh MacRaoiridh

XV *Coisich a rùin*   84

XVI Iorram do Shir Lachann (?c. 1635)   86
Mhic Moire na grèine
– Eachann Bacach

XVII *Sona do cheird, a Chalbhaigh*   90
– Cathal Mac Muireadhaigh

XVIII *A Sheónóid méadaigh meanma* (c. 1637)   94
– Cathal Mac Muireadhaigh

XIX Oran do Dhòmhnall Gorm Og, Mac Dhòmhnaill   100
    (c. 1640)
A Dhòmhnaill an Dùin
– Iain Lom

XX Oran air latha blàir Inbhir Lòchaidh (1645)   106
'N cuala sibh-se an tionndadh duineil
– Iain Lom

XXI *Turas mo chreiche thug mi Chola* (?c. 1645)   112

XXII An Cobhernandori (1648)   116
An oidhche nochd gur fada leam

XXIII *Bithidh 'n deoch-sa an làimh mo rùin*   120

XXIV Oran do Thighearna Ghrannt (c. 1645)   122
Lìon mulad mi fèin
– Seumas MacGriogair

XXV *Chailin òig as stiùramaiche*   128

XXVI Oran cumhaidh air cor na rìoghachd (1651)   130
Mi gabhail Sraith Dhruim Uachdair
– Iain Lom

XXVII Do Mhac Leòid   134
'S mòr mo mhulad 's mo phràmhan
– Màiri nighean Alasdair Ruaidh

XXVIII Fuaim an taibh   138
– Màiri nighean Alasdair Ruaidh

XXIX Oran do Mhac Mhic Raghnaill na Ceapaich   144
   (c. 1663)
Mi am shuidhe air bhruaich torrain
– Iain Lom

XXX Iorram na sgiobaireachd (?c. 1670)   148
Gur neo-shocrach mo cheum
– Murchadh Mòr

XXXI *Is garbh a-nochd an oidhch' rim' thaobh*   154
– Murchadh Mòr

XXXII Marbhrann do Mhac Gille Chaluim Ratharsaidh   156
   (1671)
Seall a-mach an e an latha e

XXXIII Moladh na pìoba   160
'S mairg do dhi-moil ceòl is caismeachd
– Gilleasbaig na Ceapaich

XXXIV *Biodh an uidheam seo triall*   162
– Iain Lom

XXXV Luinneag Mhic Neachdainn (?c. 1680)   166
'S fhad tha mi ag èisdeachd ri ur dìochuimhn

XXXVI Marbhrann Thighearna na Comraich (c. 1685)   172
An taobh tuath ud cha tèid mi

XXXVII Air dha bhith uair an Dùn Eideann   176
Ge socrach mo leaba b'annsa cadal air fraoch
– An Ciaran Mabach

XXXVIII *Rìgh na cruinne ta gun chrìch*   182
– Donnchadh nam Pìos

XXXIX Coille Chragaidh (?1691)   184
'N àm dhol sìos
– Iain mac Ailein

XL Oran murtadh Ghlinn Comhann (1692)   190
Mìle marbhaisg air an t-saoghal

XLI Oran do Mhac Leòid Dhùn Bheagain (c. 1694)   198
Miad a' mhulaid tha am thadhal
– An Clàrsair Dall

XLII Cumha Choire an Easa (c. 1696)   206
'S mi an-diugh a' fàgail na tìre
– Am Pìobaire Dall

XLIII Do Chlainn Ghill-Eain (?c. 1698)   212
Cha choma leam fhèin no co-dhiù sin
– Mairghread nighean Lachlainn

Notes   217

Glossary   239

Preface

This is a personal collection of poems and songs from the seventeenth century. It is not primarily concerned to provide texts for study, or to be even-handedly representative of all the kinds of verse extant from that century. It is a selection of the poems and songs we like best, though we do think it includes a sufficiently wide range of types to allow the reader to feel confident that the impression he/she gets of that century is a fair one. All of the songs or poems have been published in some form before, but songs in the vernacular often exist in several versions. Many of them have already been well edited, using all the available versions, but here we give only the texts of individual versions in most cases, not seeking to establish any definitive 'original' or 'complete' text of the song concerned. Sometimes this results in texts quite different from those published elsewhere, and we make no claim to having better texts, only alternative ones.

We present here the results of academic work on the period, without presenting the work itself: perhaps we will have the opportunity to publish the academic apparatus later on. The project originated with Professor Donald MacAulay, who first came up with the idea of a new anthology of Gaelic vernacular verse of the period before 1730: he has kindly allowed us to use some of the groundwork for that project as groundwork for this one. We are especially grateful to the Reverend William Matheson for his help and for permission to use the tunes he published in *Tocher* for nos I and II; for permission to use the texts of nos XXXI and XLI, first published by him, and the text of no. XVIII, first published by his late brother, Angus Matheson; also to Mrs Ena Matheson, Skye, for permission to use no. XVIII. To Dr John Lorne Campbell of Canna for permission to publish again nos V, XV, and XXV from collections published by him. To Dr Alan Bruford and the School of Scottish Studies for guidance and co-operation throughout, and for permission to reproduce the tunes of nos I, II, XX, XXIII and XXXII. To Mrs Kate Havard, London, for permission to use those of nos XX and XXXII, sung by her late father, James Campbell. We have based two of the texts (nos II and VIII) on the 1949 collection *Orain luaidh Màiri nighean Alasdair* by Kirkland C. Craig (d. 1963); but even with reasonable diligence we have failed to identify the owners of any existing copyright in that work.

We are grateful also to Miss E.B.K. Gregorson, Edinburgh, for permission to use MacNicol MS A in Edinburgh University Library for the text of nos IX and XXX; to the Special Collections Librarian there also for permission to use it, and also to use Carmichael-Watson MS 58A (for no. XXIII) and the Angus Fraser manuscript (for the tune to no. XXXIV). To the Librarian of Glasgow University for permission to use texts from the MacLagan MSS (for nos III, XXII, XXVII and XXXII). To the Trustees of the National Library of Scotland for permission to use manuscripts in their care as sources for nos XXI, XXXVI and XLII. To the Provincial Archivist, Nova Scotia, for permission to use Hector Maclean's manuscript (MG15G/2/2), our source for nos XVI, XXXIII, XXXIV and XXXIX. To Mr Hugh Barron and the Gaelic Society of Inverness for permission to print no. XXXI from their *Transactions*; to the Society of West Highland and Island Historical Research for permission to reproduce no. X from their *Notes and Queries*; and to Professor Pádraig A. Breatnach, Editor of *Éigse*, Dublin, for permission to reproduce the text of no. XVIII.

Introduction

In his *Introduction to Gaelic Poetry*, first published in 1974, Derick Thomson designated the seventeenth century as one of 'Clan and Politics'. That designation could hardly be bettered, even though there are many songs and poems from that century which would not qualify as being primarily concerned with either clan or politics. Over a whole century the range of themes will inevitably be much wider than could be encompassed within any two words, but clan and politics do figure extremely prominently in our extant poems and songs from the seventeenth century.

Writers who come to the history of the Highlands from the outside sometimes tend to see the politics of seventeenth-century verse as being merely a narrow-minded Highland politics with no national interest; and they may see the 'clan poetry' of the time as a basically negative 'anti-Campbell' poetry. As evidence it is usual to cite Iain Lom's famous song on the battle of Inverlochy (no. XX here), where the battle is portrayed basically as one fought between the MacDonalds and the Campbells, which indeed it was to a considerable extent. But poets are free to express a variety of ideas in a variety of ways, and a glance at the remainder of Iain Lom's considerable extant corpus, or at the selection in the present anthology, will show that the Gaels had as much knowledge of, and interest in, the national political world as any other group in Scotland had. Gaelic poets certainly had their own distinctive interest in their clans, but these were a fundamental distinctive feature of their social order and as such of valid concern to poets.

Like every other century, the seventeenth was one of great change in the Highlands, as in Scotland as a whole. When the century opened James Stuart, James VI, ruled Scotland, a king acceptable to all Gaels because his ancestry was traceable to the kings of Dál Riada in the fifth century, and Elizabeth ruled England; soon the Stuart family occupied the united throne of Scotland and England in London (and did not show much commitment to Scotland thereafter); but at the end of the century that throne was occupied by William of Orange and there was never to be a Stuart king again. When the century opened, as far as we know, the poetry accorded prestige was the medieval syllabic verse of highly learned and literate professional poets, using the Classical standard Gaelic which had been the norm in both Scotland and Ireland for four hundred years; but by the end of the century that old learned tradition of poetry had virtually come to an end, and been replaced by the new, fundamentally non-literate, song tradition in vernacular Scottish Gaelic. This new song tradition is marked by regular stress, a clear 'beat', the sort of thing we expect in a modern song, whether in Gaelic or in English. But the medieval syllabic verse was centred on the number of syllables in the line, and regularity of rhythm was apparently of no interest: it is perhaps hard for a modern reader even to imagine what its audience found attractive about syllabic verse.

All in all, with political, social and metrical changes, the seventeenth century probably was in many ways one of greater change than most.

The Statutes of Iona

Before the seventeenth century began, James VI was already busy trying to extend his effective rule in the Highlands, where he considered the people barbarous and their Gaelic language more so. Despite the official promulgation of the Reformation in 1560 many Highlanders had not yet changed their religion, and Edinburgh found their Roman Catholicism as objectionable as their language.

The parliament in 1597 passed an Act requiring Highland chiefs to produce their title-deeds, and since the MacLeods of Lewis, Sìol Torcaill, could not provide the documentation of their title to their lands in Lewis, Skye and the mainland, they forfeited their title to the lands. Sìol Torcaill had already been torn between rival claimants to their chiefship, one of whom is said to have conveyed the family papers for safe-keeping to

MacKenzie of Kintail. In 1597 Torcall Dubh, one of the MacLeod contenders, was captured (by Uisdean Breitheamh, a leader of the Morrisons, it is said) and handed over to his half-brother, Torcall Conanach, to be executed. It has been suggested that our song no. I refers to the actions of Niall (known to oral tradition as Niall Odhar), another claimant to the MacLeod inheritance, as he sought revenge on the Morrisons for this.

Ian Grimble offers a concise assessment of the king's attitude to Lewis at the time: 'James was, in fact, motivated by a somewhat lunatic racial prejudice against the Gaels. He was also a victim of the delusion that peaty Lewis was extremely fertile, and this perhaps helped him to decide that the solution to the problem of ownership was to exterminate all its inhabitants and settle Lowlanders in their place.'[1]

The lands were granted in 1598 to a group of twelve Lowland colonists, usually known as the Fife Adventurers, and as the seventeenth century opened these adventurers were being vigorously opposed by MacLeods, MacDonalds and MacKenzies. Supported by the king, who in 1603 succeeded to the English throne and moved to London, the adventurers were able to hold on to the land for some years; but local opposition prevented much development of the land and in 1609 they were finally bought out by Coinneach, Lord MacKenzie of Kintail (1569–1611), who took over the control of Lewis with the help of Niall Odhar.[2] Historians today sometimes portray the MacKenzie takeover in terms of rescuing the island from the feuding and unChristian barbarities of uncivilised MacLeods; but then history is seldom written by the losers. The MacKenzies remained in favour with the king, and in 1623 Coinneach's son, Cailean Ruadh, was made the first Earl of Seaforth.

The MacKenzies were not the only clan leaders used by the king to exercise his control over other clans. James intervened in a long-standing feud between the MacGregors and the Campbells of Glenorchy by issuing various 'commissions' to the latter's close relative, Gilleasbaig Gruamach (1575–1638), 7th Earl of Argyll, to reduce the MacGregors to obedience. Some of the enactments were extremely severe and in 1603, just before the king went off to England, the name of MacGregor itself became illegal. Persecution and pursuit of MacGregors continued well into the seventeenth century, and indeed the law outlawing their name

remained in effect until 1775, when it was noted that it had finally
fallen out of practical use.[3]

As a reward for his success against the MacGregors,
Gilleasbaig Gruamach was in 1607 given royal title to the lands
of Clann Iain Mhòir, the MacDonalds of Dùn Naomhaig in Islay,
and some of the documents of these affairs reflect an intense
anti-MacDonald animus on Argyll's part. The lands Clann Iain
Mhòir had held for hundreds of years, and were now expelled
from, included Kintyre, Islay and Jura, and the Campbell takeover
was facilitated by ferocious disagreement between the MacDon-
ald leader, Aonghas, and his son, Sir James. Their fortress, Dùn
Naomhaig, was surrendered in 1608 by Sir James' brother,
Aonghas Og, to Andrew Stewart (1560–1628), Lord Ochiltree,
who was leading an expedition to the Isles on behalf of the king
and the Privy Council. Clann Iain Mhòir can be said to have lost
everything except for the Irish lands held by their junior branch,
the Macdonnells of Antrim. One important aspect of the Camp-
bell takeover was their acquisition of Colonsay, where the local
MacDonald leader was Colla Ciotach (c. 1570–1647). Colla and
Aonghas Og captured Dùn Naomhaig in 1614, but Campbell of
Calder attacked it and in 1615 Colla fled. He then became
something of a pirate, plundering ships which plied between
Ireland and Scotland, before accepting Argyll's superiority in
Colonsay. His son Alasdair, born in Colonsay about 1610, was
to lead a last great attempt to restore Clann Iain Mhòir in 1644.[4]

Feuds of various kinds between different clans continued, and
even if they did not gain historical importance by being made use
of by the king, they often have importance in the context of Gaelic
song. A long-standing feud between the MacKenzies and the
MacDonalds of Glengarry, largely concerning the title to lands
in south-west Ross, had been dormant for some time, but came
to a head with large-scale raids, in both directions, in 1601 and
after. In 1603 Ailean mac Raghnaill, MacDonald of Lundy near
Invergarry (the subject of our no. IV), a close relative of Glen-
garry, raided MacKenzie lands at Cille Chrìosd (Tarradale) in
Easter Ross, killing at least five people and causing great destruc-
tion. Tradition has it that a whole MacKenzie congregation in
the church was burnt to death, but the historical evidence for that
is not good. The feud seems to have come to an end almost
immediately.[5]

We have a considerable body of traditional lore on a feud which developed around 1600 between Sìol Tormaid, the MacLeods of Harris and Dunvegan, and the MacDonalds of Sleat. Whatever the original cause of the feud (and the generally accepted account reads as much like a folktale as like history), it resulted in the battle of Carinish in North Uist (part of the Sleat territory) in or around 1601, in which a small party of MacDonalds, led by Dòmhnall mac Iain mhic Sheumais (d.c. 1660), defeated a small raiding party of MacLeods. But Mac Iain mhic Sheumais was wounded, and this gave rise to our song no. II.[6]

Edinburgh's efforts to control the Highlanders were already being redoubled, and we have seen that the government had an expedition by sea under Lord Ochiltree in 1608, when he accepted the surrender of Dùn Naomhaig by the MacDonalds. Ochiltree went on then to Mull, where he summoned twelve of the principal Highland chiefs on board to hear a sermon from Andrew Knox, Bishop of the Isles and commissioner for the king. But the chiefs were kidnapped and taken to Lowland prisons, where most of them were kept over the winter. In August 1609 they were released on condition that they attend a meeting in Iona with Bishop Knox, and sign the nine 'Statutes of Iona', designed to contribute to the civilisation and deGaelicisation of the Highlands, as well as to further the Reformation there. After measures to control fornication, adultery, Highland hospitality and excessive drinking, the sixth statute states:

> It is inactit that everie gentilman or yeaman
> within the said Ilandis, or ony of thame, haveing
> childreine maill or famell, and being in goodis
> worth thriescore ky, sall put at the leist thair
> eldest sone, or haveing no childrene maill thair
> eldest dochter, to the scuillis on the Lawland, and
> interteny and bring thame up thair quhill thay may
> be found able sufficientlie to speik, reid, and
> wryte Inglische . . .

to which the eighth statute adds:

> It is lykwyse inactit . . . that na vagabound, baird,
> nor profest pleisant pretending libertie to baird

and flattir, be ressavit within the boundis of the
saidis Yllis be ony of the saidis speciall barronis
and gentilmen or ony utheris inhabitantis thairof,
or interteneit, be thame or ony of thame in ony
soirt; but, incais ony vagaboundis, bairdis,
juglouris, or suche lyke be apprehendit be thame or
ony of thame, he to be tane and put in suir
fensment and keiping in the stokis, and thaireafter
to be debarit furth of the cuntrey with all guidlie
expeditioun . . . [7]

What exactly the drafters of this meant by the term *baird* is
perhaps open to question, but they clearly found Gaelic poets, of
some kind, to be a menace to good Edinburgh government, just
as their language was. The Gaelic professional poets, as we will
see, were to a large extent the political brains behind the High-
land chiefs' military strength, and probably the authorities were
right to be afraid of them.

The Statutes were not, in the end, very effective in forcing the
Highland leaders to abide by all they signed; if our no. VII is, as
is thought, an account of a wedding in Dunvegan in 1613, the
strictures on 'strong wynis' in the fifth statute had perhaps not
been taken deeply to heart. But the elaborate planning of the 1608
kidnap, and the force used to have the Statutes signed, mark what
David Stevenson calls the 'maturing' of government intervention
in the Highlands: pressure on the Gaels is now increased with
more frequent expeditions like Ochiltree's, and with 'the intro-
duction of policies which would reform Highland society and, in
time, remodel it on Lowland lines.'[8] By the time the Statutes were
ratified by the Privy Council in 1616 the chiefs were already
becoming more submissive to the decrees of government, and
the Council now felt free to be very much more offensive in the
expression of their view that Gaelic must 'be abolisheit and
removit'.

The deGaelicisation of Ulster

The increasingly effective control of Gaeldom in Scotland by the
government is paralleled and reinforced by very similar develop-
ments in Ireland around the same time. The Tudor effort to

assert London control over all of Ireland achieved success at the battle of Kinsale in 1601. There Queen Elizabeth's English forces defeated Irish and Spanish forces, the Irish leaders being the Ulster chiefs O Neill, Earl of Tyrone, O Donnell, Earl of Tyrconnell (Tír Chonaill) and Maguire of Fermanagh. Ulster was the last great virtually independent Gaelic region in Ireland, and the defeat of Kinsale has long been seen, perhaps rather too simply, as the downfall of the Gaelic world in Ireland. But it was the beginning of the end, and the rest of the seventeenth century continued the process. The older Gaelic way of life involved, among many other distinctive features, a system in which independent clan leaders maintained a class of hereditary learned poets who were important to them as political advisers and sources of learning, and who depended on the chiefs for their living. With the defeat of Kinsale and later developments the chiefs ceased to have any power and could not maintain the poets, so that the whole four-hundred-year-old tradition of professional syllabic poetry comes to an end. It is reckoned that the last school in Ireland which trained these poets must have closed its doors around 1640. It is, however, important to remember, for it is often forgotten (especially in Ireland), that Scotland had no Kinsale, and the old Gaelic way of life survived here for another century and a half.

The Ulster chiefs came to an accommodation with London, just as the new king, James VI, took up his English throne in 1603: they continued to hold their lands, but it was now by the grace of the king. They held on for some time, but in 1607 a body of over one hundred Gaels, including O Neill and O Donnell, slipped away from Ireland secretly by ship for the continent (no one yet knows quite why), and the old Gaelic world in Ireland was manifestly over.

This was 'the Flight of the Earls', remembered as one of the saddest days in Irish history. It was followed by the Plantation of Ulster, according to a plan first published in 1609, whereby most of the best lands in six of the Ulster counties were given to settlers from England and Lowland Scotland. The natives were to be left with the poorer land, or to become servants or tenants to the settlers. One of the counties which was not planted was Antrim, which was already in what might be considered Scottish hands: MacDonnell of Antrim played his cards well and in 1620 king James made him Earl of Antrim. (One of the earlier 'undertakers'

in the Ulster plantation, who took charge of lands in Tyrone in
1610, was the same Andrew Stewart, Lord Ochiltree, who, as the
king's lieutenant, had played such a large part in forcing the
Highland chiefs to sign the Statutes of Iona.)

The plantation of Ulster took many years longer than was at
first envisaged, and Gaels remained a much larger percentage of
the people than had been intended, but Highland leaders were
now effectively deprived of contact with any Irish counterparts:
for centuries Irish and Highland chiefs had fought together in a
variety of causes. The strong link of a professional class of poets,
with their common literary standard language, was also soon
broken. It is in the early seventeenth century that we really begin
to find a body of extant literature, mainly songs, in the Scottish
Gaelic vernacular, taking their place beside the Classical Gaelic
verse which they were to replace. Add to all this the fact that many
in the Highlands had adopted, or were to adopt, the Reformation,
decreed in 1560, while the Irish Gaels set their faces against it
from an early date, and it looks as if the old cultural unity of the
Gaelic world has been destroyed. From the early seventeenth
century Scottish Gaeldom is on its own.[9]

King Charles I, Alasdair mac Colla and Montrose

James VI is generally reckoned one of the most effective and
successful of Scotland's kings, not least for his success in impos-
ing his will on the Highlands. But his ambition from an early stage
had been to become king of England as well, and after he
achieved that in 1603 he returned to Scotland only once, for three
months in 1617. Perhaps he is to blame to some extent for the
jaundiced view of the Highlands held by his son Charles I, who
succeeded him in 1625. Already in 1626 Charles (in London) was
signing orders aimed at 'the better civilising and removing of the
Irish language and barbaritie out of the heighlands', and in 1629
he writes of an agreement reached with some chiefs in the
Highlands to carry out a plantation in Nova Scotia (inspired by
the success of the Plantation of Ulster) 'for debordening that our
kingdome of that race of people, which in former times hade bred
so many troubles ther'. Even so, Charles soon lost interest in
'civilising' the Highlanders, who were eventually to become his
most prominent supporters.[10]

In or around 1630 there was published in Edinburgh a translation into Classical Gaelic of John Calvin's *Catechismus Ecclesiae Genevensis* (1545). This serves as a useful reminder, in the context, that there were those among the Gaels who had the confidence, and the resources, to see that Gaelic had a part to play in the furtherance of the Reformation in the Highlands. The Campbell Earls of Argyll, supporters of kings against other Highlanders, were among the most prominent of Scotland's reformers, and the first Gaelic book ever printed was John Carswell's *Foirm na n-Urrnuidheadh* (Edinburgh 1567), a translation into Classical Gaelic of John Knox's *Book of Common Order*: the translator owed his position as Bishop of the Isles to the Earl of Argyll. It was in Argyllshire too, probably, that Calvin's *Catechism* was translated, perhaps by a member of the MacMharcuis learned family in Kintyre, or by one of the MacEòghainn (MacEwan) learned family, poets to the Earls of Argyll. The idea that Gaelic had to be 'extirpated' first, in order that the Gaels could read the Bible in English, though certainly in existence in the seventeenth century, did not really come out into the ecclesiastical open until the eighteenth. Throughout the second half of the seventeenth century it was the Synod of Argyll, strongly sponsored by the Campbells, who led the way in the publication of religious literature in Gaelic.[11]

While the Argyll family could and did provide resources for the printing and publication of religious material in Gaelic, there was no money for secular literature. Therefore all the other prose, like the classical poetry, which survives from the seventeenth century has come down to us in manuscript form. The classical Gaelic tradition of manuscript-writing continued throughout the century in parallel with the classical tradition of poetry. A recent account of the classical Gaelic manuscripts, written in the old Gaelic hand, shows a sustained input by Scottish scribes throughout the century, as they copied and reordered wide ranges of earlier and contemporary literary, medical and other material. Not only the tradition, but even the manuscripts themselves, give clear evidence of strong Irish links; and more classical manuscripts are extant from the seventeenth than from any other century.[12]

The classical tradition, however, grew weaker under pressure during the course of the century, and so also, it seems, did the chiefs' commitment to their hereditary role as leaders and patrons of the Gaels. It is well known that the deGaelicisation of the Highland chiefs, well documented after Culloden, was already under way in the late seventeenth century, and our no. XLI is a well-known response of the 1690s to a MacLeod chief's turning his back on his lands and using them to finance a Lowland lifestyle. But Allan Macinnes[13] has made the interesting suggestion that in no. XVI here Sir Lachlann Maclean of Duart is being gently chided by his poet for doing the same thing already in the 1630s. Sir Lachlann was one of the baronets of Nova Scotia under king Charles' scheme of the 1620s: it is not at all unlikely that he would have ideas of luxury beyond what was available in his clan homeland in Mull.

Naturally hopeful of unifying his new joint kingdom, James VI had tried in various ways to nudge the Scottish church towards the Episcopalianism which was the mark of the church in England. But Charles was much less sensitive than his father to the Scottish church and preferred to enforce his will: in 1637 he had a new Service-book published for the Scottish church, and because it was so similar to Episcopal practice it caused uproar. Large numbers of people opposed it vigorously and in 1638 the National Covenant was framed, the signatories, the 'Covenanters', pledging themselves to defend the king but to reject his Episcopalian decrees.

But of course many people were opposed to the Covenant; before the end of 1638 Raghnall, the second Earl of Antrim, indicated his support for the king, pointing out that the MacDonalds in general had refused to sign it. A few months later Gilleasbaig Caoch (1607–1661), 8th Earl of Argyll, who was to become Scotland's leading Covenanter, signed the Covenant. The king was forced to allow a General Assembly, which forthwith abolished Episcopacy, and the Scottish Parliament confirmed its abolition in 1640. A Scottish army marched into England and forced the king to sign a treaty accepting the abolition of Episcopacy and giving the parliament the right to challenge the king's ministers; among the leaders of this Covenanting army was James Graham (1612–1650), Earl of Montrose.

In the same year the English parliament also asserted itself, forcing the king to accept the unthinkable – that he could not control parliament in every way – and as a result England slipped towards civil war. In Ireland the Gaels in Ulster in 1641 attacked the lands taken over in the Plantation and large numbers of the Scots and English settlers – how large the numbers were is still a matter of dispute – were killed. The leaders hoped to take control of Ulster, then Dublin, and then to join with other Catholics to exact a guarantee of religious liberty from the government. Late in 1641 Alasdair mac Colla Chiotaich, whose father had resisted the Campbell conquest of Clann Iain Mhòir in 1614, emerges as a military leader and joins the Gaelic Irish insurrection. David Stevenson argues that it was in a minor battle in County Antrim in 1642 that Alasdair 'invented' what became known as the 'Highland charge', leading his 'rebels' to defeat a Protestant force which had made a sortie from Coleraine. Shortly afterwards a Scottish army was sent to Ulster to defend the Scots there, and the English sent troops to Dublin, while the 'Catholic Confederacy' grew and began its long war against Dublin and the English.

Late in 1642 the Earl of Antrim saw a way of linking the wars in Scotland, Ireland and England together so that the king might defeat the English parliament and his other enemies, including the Covenanters. In 1643 the Earl of Montrose finally broke with the Covenant and joined the king's side and, in consultation with the king and Montrose, Antrim commissioned Alasdair mac Colla to lead an army from Ireland to Scotland. Meanwhile the Covenanters of Scotland and the English parliamentarians negotiated the 'Solemn League and Covenant', bringing the Scots army into the English war against the king, in return for the spreading of the Presbyterian form of religion to England.

About 2000 men, Scots as well as Irish, sailed in June 1644 under the leadership of Alasdair mac Colla from County Wexford to Ardnamurchan, formerly MacDonald territory but now held by Campbells. The expected support from the main Highland leaders did not materialise at first, and Alasdair used force to raise Highlanders for his army as he marched east and met James Graham, now Marquis of Montrose, in Atholl. Montrose now became the leader of the army, with the king's commission, and Alasdair his lieutenant-general. For over a year the combined army marched all over central and eastern Scotland, winning six major battles against Covenanting armies and, in the winter of

1644–45, carrying out a horrifying conquest of Argyll and slaughter of Campbells. Niall MacMhuirich, *seanchaidh* to the Clanranald chiefs and the last of his learned line, is quite happy to report that 895 men were killed in the lands of Mac Cailein that winter, without any battle taking place.[14]

Perhaps the best known of the six battles is that of Inverlochy, fought on February 2nd, 1645, at what is now Fort William, after Alasdair's army had left Argyll and was followed into Lochaber by a Covenanting (mainly Campbell) force. The defeat of the Covenanters there is celebrated by Iain Lom in our song no. XX, where the battle is presented as a MacDonald versus Campbell one, and Montrose does not rate a mention. Practically all the vernacular Gaelic song we have from this period views it from the Royalist/MacDonald/Montrose side, though our no. XXI seems to offer a rare Campbell viewpoint. Montrose's amazingly successful campaign ended with defeat by the Covenanting army under David Leslie at the battle of Philiphaugh, near Selkirk, on 13th September, 1645, while Alasdair and part of the army were raiding again in Argyll and hoping to raise more recruits.[15]

Montrose himself escaped the slaughter at Philiphaugh and fled to the Highlands to continue organising resistance. But the king in 1646 threw himself on the mercy of the Scots army in England and sent an order to Montrose to disband his remaining force: Montrose did so and went into exile. The Scots army did not know what to do with their king, so they asked him if he would make Presbyterianism the religion of England. He refused, and they handed him over to the English parliament, who had failed to observe the terms of the Solemn League and Covenant, and then the army withdrew to Scotland. Alasdair mac Colla and his followers remained in Kintyre, ravaging the lands now held by Campbells, until the Covenanting army, accompanied by Gilleasbaig Caoch, followed them there in 1647. Alasdair then went to Islay and thence back to Ireland, where he was killed in November 1647, fighting for the Catholic Confederacy at Cnoc na nOs, the biggest battle ever fought in Munster.

When he left Islay, Alasdair left his father, Colla Ciotach, in command of Dùn Naomhaig, where he was besieged and forced to surrender. Argyll then tried and hanged him, it is said from the mast of his own galley, which was placed in a cleft of a rock near Dunstaffnage. It is also said that Islay people still regard

Alasdair with contempt, because he abandoned his men there.[16]

In 1647 some members of the Scottish parliament signed a treaty, known as the 'Engagement', by which they agreed to take the side of king Charles if he would support Presbyterianism in England for three years. Many Scots disapproved, but in 1648 James Hamilton, 1st Duke of Hamilton, led an army of 'Engagers' into England, where they were defeated at Preston by a much smaller English army led by Oliver Cromwell and John Lambert. It seems likely that our song no. XXII refers to this unsuccessful compromise.[17]

Early in 1649 the English executed Charles I, and the way was clear for Cromwell's parliamentary rule. But Cromwell was not willingly accepted in Scotland, mainly because of the execution of the king. Montrose returned from exile in the Netherlands to carry out an invasion for Charles' son Charles, but his small force was easily defeated at Carbisdale in Easter Ross in April 1650. He himself escaped, but was betrayed two days later by Niall MacLeod of Assynt, and taken to Edinburgh where he was hanged in May.[18] The outlook must then have looked bleak for the Royalist Highlanders, who had now lost both their great leaders, Alasdair mac Colla and Montrose, and must have seen both the Scottish parliament and Cromwell's English army as their bitter enemies: Iain Lom paints a very bleak picture in our no. XXVI.

Cromwell, King Charles II and James VII

But Cromwell and the Covenanters were no longer on the same side. In 1650 Cromwell led his army into Scotland, defeating David Leslie's Scots army at Dunbar, and took control in Edinburgh. Charles II was crowned king at Scone on January 1st 1651 and, though he had no power, he was a symbol round which resistance to Cromwell gathered. Highlanders who had fought for Charles I against the Covenanters were now admitted to the ranks of the Scottish (Covenanters') army fighting Cromwell. Considerable numbers of the MacLeods, Macleans and Buchanans joined the army led by Leslie. In July 1651, while Leslie held Stirling to keep Cromwell from moving north, Cromwell's army crossed the Forth into Fife, led by General John Lambert, and Leslie sent part of his army, including the Macleans and Buchanans, to meet them at Inverkeithing. Lambert won the battle there and most of the Macleans and Buchanans were killed, including Eachann Ruadh, the chief of Duart.[19] Leslie and the king then led their army into England and Cromwell followed. They met on August 22nd 1651 at the battle of Worcester, where Cromwell was victorious; the MacLeod contingent of about 700 men was virtually wiped out, though its leaders, Sir Tormod of Berneray (subject of our no. XXVIII) and his brother, Sir Ruaidhri of Talisker, managed to escape.[20]

Cromwell was now firmly in control. An uprising led by William Cunningham, Earl of Glencairn, in 1653, and involving, among other Highlanders, Eòghann Cameron of Lochiel, Aonghas MacDonald of Glengarry and Gilleasbaig Fionn, son of the Marquis of Argyll, was effectively, but with admirable restraint, put down in 1654 by General George Monk (1608–1670), who ruled Scotland for Cromwell until 1660, building castles at Inverlochy (later Fort William) and Inverness to assert his authority.[21]

In the peace that follows we find the Synod of Argyll continuing its work of Gaelic publication. In 1653 they published a Gaelic translation of the General Assembly's *Shorter Catechism* (on which they had been working since 1649); they printed it again in 1659 along with the first fifty of the metrical Psalms in Gaelic (these translated to fit Lowland tunes foreign to the Gaels). This was the first appearance of any section of the Old Testament in Gaelic print. In both cases the language is basically the Classical written language, as adapted by Carswell, but R.L. Thomson has pointed to considerable influence from the Scottish Gaelic vernacular in both, more especially in the *Shorter Catechism*.[22]

With the Restoration of the monarchy in the person of Charles II in 1660, the Episcopalian form of church government was established and firmly imposed and the Presbyterian Synod of Argyll, with its work in Gaelic translation and publishing, fades into obscurity. Gilleasbaig Caoch, Marquis of Argyll, who had fought so long for the Covenant against Charles I, was put on trial for treason, one of the crimes cited against him being the killing of Colla Ciotach in 1647. On 27 May 1661 Mac Cailein was beheaded by the famous 'Maiden', a kind of guillotine, in Edinburgh.

In our no. XXIX we have a good example of a 'clan' song which (like many of the praise poems of the century) has nothing much to do with national politics. Though it amounts (in our version) to an elegy for a dead clan chief and little more, it is one of a group of five or six songs by Iain Lom related to the Keppoch Murder of 1663, when Alasdair, the young chief of the MacDonalds of Keppoch, and his brother Raghnall were murdered by some of their own kin. The murder of a chief was apparently an extremely rare occurrence in the Highlands, yet the Keppoch clan seem to have had little interest in bringing the guilty to justice. Iain Lom therefore became very unpopular among them when he took on the role of avenger, doubtless because he was conscious of the traditional political duties of a poet. We have songs addressed by him to Sir Seumas MacDonald of Sleat and Aonghas of Glengarry (now Lord MacDonell and Aros), whom he sought to persuade to apprehend the murderers. In the end it was Sir Seumas who took action: he got a commission of fire and sword from the Privy Council in 1665 and delegated it to his brother Gilleasbaig, An Ciaran Mabach (author of our no. XXXVII), who saw to it that some, at least, of the guilty were beheaded. Tradition tells us that it was Iain Lom himself who guided An Ciaran Mabach to the murderers' house.[23]

In 1663 Gilleasbaig Fionn, now 9th Earl of Argyll, set diligently about buying up Maclean debts, in order to continue a process, which may have begun as far back as the 1630s, of legal acquisition of the Maclean lands by the House of Argyll. After the earl's execution in 1685 various Macleans joined other Highlanders in raiding and plundering in Argyllshire, but the new earl, Gilleasbaig Beag, resolutely pursued the campaign against the Maclean assets by invading Mull in October 1690. The Maclean chief, Sir Iain, fled to the fortified island of Ceàrnaburg, but in March 1691 he was forced to hand over his castles, and the superiority of his lands, to Argyll.[24] This was a terrible blow to the pride of the Macleans and their poets, and our no. XLIII reflects something close to shock that, after all these years of Campbell success and prosperity at the expense of the Macleans, the wheel of fortune has as yet failed to turn and bring the Macleans back to the glory of the distant past.

For Scotland as a whole the only serious trouble during the 1670s was the solid resistance of the Covenanters of the south-west to the imposition of Epicopalianism there. This led to blows at times, and the government's short-sighted overreactions to disaffection inevitably kept the trouble brewing. In 1678 their reaction was to send into the south-west a force of militia with a 6000-man 'Highland host'. These men were mainly from the eastern Highlands, from Perthshire to Inverness, and they were used to overawe the Covenanters for a month – no doubt exacerbating the prejudices which divided Highlander and Lowlander.

Captain John Graham of Claverhouse (1648–1689) appears on the scene at Drumclog in Ayrshire in 1679, where his force of professional soldiers was routed by the Covenanters. In 1680 a group of fighting men was formed by the preacher Richard Cameron, to make war on the king and defend the Covenant; this drew the government's wrath on the 'Cameronians', some of whose later adherents were to be accepted into the army as a fully-fledged regiment, but it also led to a fading away of popular support for the more extreme Covenanters.[25]

In the world of Gaelic publishing at this time we find one outstanding minister of the established (Episcopalian) church, the Rev. Robert Kirk, or Kirke (1644–1692), minister of Balquhidder in Perthshire, who in 1684 published in Edinburgh a complete text of the Gaelic metrical Psalms, using the first fifty published in 1659 but providing the text for the other hundred himself. The work of translation had been completed by 1673 and must have been an enormous undertaking (it had taken at least four translators six years to produce the first fifty). We are told that Kirk 'sat up the greater part of the night for many months' to get his version of the last hundred Psalms finished ahead of the version which had been begun by the Presbyterian clergy before the Restoration: such a huge undertaking, as we will see, was fully in keeping with Kirk's character. Possibly because he was an Episcopalian, histories of the Gaelic Bible generally give little credit to Kirk's Psalter. One commentator writes: 'This version found no favour in Gaelic-speaking parishes; indeed there is no proof that it was ever used in any church.'[26]

In 1685 Charles II died and was succeeded by his brother James VII, who was a Roman Catholic. Even with his policy of a degree of toleration for non-Episcopalians, James' succession was widely accepted. The most dramatic move made in Scotland against his succession was the arrival of Gilleasbaig Fionn, 9th Earl of Argyll, from exile in Holland to lead a rebellion against James. But the rebellion was botched and Mac Cailein was beheaded in Edinburgh on 30 June 1685.

King William

When king James' son James was born in 1688 it became obvious that a Roman Catholic succession to the throne was now more than likely. Many people, especially in England, were disturbed by this prospect and a swelling of opinion against James there led to openly-canvassed support for Prince William of Orange, James' son-in-law, to succeed as king. Under pressure, James fled to France and William took the kingship. The considerable numbers of remaining supporters of James (and, later, of his son) are known as the Jacobites.

In 1689 James went to Ireland, where there was strong Jacobite support, and took part in the long and unsuccessful Siege of Derry, while on 11th April 1689 William and his wife Mary Stuart were proclaimed king and queen of Scotland. James' Scottish supporters came together under the leadership of John Graham of Claverhouse, now Viscount Dundee (he was a distant relative of the Marquis of Montrose), and on 27th July 1689 the Jacobite defeat of a Williamite army at Killiecrankie was probably the most dramatic success of the 'Highland charge'. It is celebrated in song by Iain Lom and, in our no. XXXIX, by the Maclean poet Iain mac Ailein.

The victory of Killiecrankie, however, was cancelled out by the death there of Dundee, and shortly afterwards the Jacobite army was defeated by a much smaller force of Cameronians in Dunkeld. The Jacobite reaction in arms to William's arrival was thus effectively almost over in Scotland, and in 1690 William established the Church of Scotland as a Presbyterian one again.[27]

The Gaelic Bible had been completed with the publication in Ireland in 1685 of the Old Testament, translated into Classical Gaelic by a team directed and inspired by the English-born bishop William Bedell. The print used had been based on the old Gaelic script, used for centuries for manuscripts in both Scotland and Ireland; but Gaelic print in Scotland had always used the common Roman-style print used also in English. So copies of Bedell's Old Testament sent over to Scotland in 1688 do not

seem to have been well received, and it was arranged that Robert
Kirk should transcribe the entire Gaelic Bible for Roman print.
He carried out this prodigious work single-handed within eigh-
teen months and his Bible, the first complete Gaelic Bible ever
printed, was published in London on 1st April 1690 – just as the
Episcopalian church, to which both Kirk and his Bible belonged,
was being disestablished in Scotland. That disestablishment may
be to some extent responsible for the fact that Kirk's Bible was
never widely accepted in Scotland, and even today it is referred
to as an 'Irish' Bible. This designation is correct in that it was
translated in Ireland, for the (Episcopalian) Church of Ireland.
But the language is not merely 'Irish': it is, as far as we know, the
Classical Gaelic of Carswell (1567) and the 1630 *Calvin's Cate-
chism*: a good deal of detailed study, both of the language itself
and of the extent of Gaelic literacy in the Highlands, will be
necessary before we can be sure that political reasons were not
as important as linguistic ones in the rejection of Kirk's Bible by
the Church of Scotland.[28] They also rejected his 1684 completed
translation of the metrical Psalms, and had their own version
published in Edinburgh in 1694.

Following the defeat of the Scottish Jacobites in 1689, William
went to Ireland in 1690 and his army met James' there at the
battle of the Boyne on 1st July. This battle, together with the 1691
Treaty of Limerick, decisively ended the Jacobite threat to Wil-
liam, and his throne looked secure. That is why the Massacre of
Glencoe, on 13 February 1692, was a serious mistake for him,
whoever we may blame for it. Both the nature and the importance
of this event have perhaps been distorted over time: it was not
part of any Campbell-MacDonald feud and it was not concerned
in any serious way with religion (indeed, historians do not seem
to be in complete agreement yet as to whether the MacDonalds
of Glencoe were Roman Catholics or Episcopalians). Only some
38 people were killed (some by the soldiers, some by the cold
weather as they fled), an extremely small number in comparison
with other seventeenth-century massacres which better deserve
the name. The peculiar notoriety of this massacre may be partly
due to its having the king's approval at a time of growing interest
in democracy. King William signed the order for it and various
figures in the chain of command have been identified, so that
blame can be apportioned, right down to the soldiers themselves,

very few of them Campbells, who carried out the killing. It is usual now to see the impetus for the massacre as originating with John Dalrymple, Master of Stair, the king's Secretary of State for Scotland, who had a fierce antipathy towards the Highlanders, but considerable blame is sometimes laid also on Iain Glas, chief of the Campbells of Breadalbane.[29]

Iain Lom saw the treacherous massacre, where the soldiers had been billeted in the Glencoe family homes for a fortnight before killing their hosts, as just another in a series of Campbell crimes; and the poet of our no. XL laments the fallen Glencoe heroes in traditional style, but sees no great national significance in the deed. It probably was not intrinsically a major turning point, but in conjunction with what Lowland leaders had seen the Campbells of Argyll doing to the Macleans it became linked in the minds of many of them with a pattern of Campbell tyranny. Since the Campbells were Williamites, this ill feeling was soon directed also at the king, who had signed the Glencoe order, and the ill feeling increased through the 1690s as Scotland's crops repeatedly failed between 1695 and 1699 and as William was blamed for betraying the Scottish scheme for a national trading colony in Darien (in Panama) in 1698–1700. As a result of the growing distaste for William, the Jacobite cause was enabled to survive, to make its major impact in the eighteenth century.

POETS AND POETRY

Professor Thomson sees the seventeenth century as a 'crucible' for Gaelic poetry[30]. It was a time of mixture of poetic traditions, some very old and some in the process of being developed and/or borrowed. It is possible to distinguish various types of poetry, and the various types of poet who composed them, and it seems to us that the most important distinction is that between, on the one hand, song (verse intended to be sung) and, on the other hand, verse which we have in the form of written art only, whether or not it was originally intended for recitation and/or harp accompaniment.

Professional syllabic poetry

The old social system which, since about 1200, had maintained a limited hereditary class of professional encomiastic poets was still apparently strong in 1600, but the century saw the decline and loss of this poetic elite, and their poetry; the last exponent, Niall MacMhuirich, died in 1726. This old learned tradition had developed and exploited a highly learned and formal literary dialect of Gaelic (which we call Classical Gaelic), and this too, to a large extent, disappears with the Classical professional poetry: the Scottish Gaelic vernacular, the language of the ordinary people, comes clearly into view for the first time in the poetry of the seventeenth century – which is, above all else, song.

Our nos VII and XVIII represent the remarkable metrical complexity of the strict form of professional syllabic poetry, known to the poets themselves as *dán díreach*, which was declining fast in the seventeenth century. The final stanza of no. VII is a good illustration of the complexity of ornament which the metre *rannaigheacht mhór* (one of a sizeable range of metres), in its strict form, imposed on the poet:

> Fiche meisge linn gach laoi –
>   nochar leisge linn ná lé;
> fiú i neart ar mbeathaidh do bhí,
>   ceathair, a trí, a seacht le sé.

The rules here require seven syllables per line, and there are rules for elision so that when two vowels occur together (in certain circumstances) one of them is elided and therefore only one syllable is counted: here we elide the word *i* in line 3 and the word *a* following *trí* in line 4. The final words of lines 2 and 4 must rhyme together (as in all rhymes, the vowels must be identical); and the vowels of the finals of all four lines must agree in 'quantity' (*i.e.* long or short), as they do here: *laoi* has a single long vowel. Internal rhyme (which in Gaelic means rhyme within the *couplet*) occurs twice in each couplet, giving us the rhymes *meisge: leisge* and *linn: linn* in the first couplet; in the second couplet the rhymes *mbeathaidh: ceathair* and *neart: seacht* are also 'perfect', because of complex Gaelic rules of consonant grouping whereby, in rhyme, -*dh*- and -*r*- belong to the same group, and the consonant 'clusters' -*rt* and -*cht* (by even more complicated rules) rhyme together. (Anything as simple as the popular English rhyming system, where *bill* rhymes with *fill* but not with *fin*, would probably have been regarded by these poets as childish.) The metre of this poem, *rannaigheacht mhór*, also demands *aicill*, a rhyme between the final of line 3 and a non-final word in line 4, here provided in the rhyme *bhí: trí*. Every line must contain at least one alliteration, as between *linn* and *laoi* in line 1 (the unstressed word *gach*, like all unstressed words, is ignored for the purpose of alliteration), and there is a double alliteration in line 2; in line 3 the alliteration between *mbeathaidh* and *bhí* demonstrates the very literate familiarity of the poets with the Gaelic conventions of mutation, *mb-* and *bh-* both being mutated forms of *b-*. For line 4 of all quatrains a further rule states that the alliteration must occur between the last two stressed words (*seacht* and *sé*).

All these rules leave the poet with very little room for manoeuvre in the matter of conveying meaning (not to mention feeling); apart from unstressed words (which must still be taken into the syllable-count) the above quatrain contains only two words, *Fiche* and *fiú*, which are not firmly bound to other words by some form of rhyme or alliteration. Years of concentrated training were necessary to teach the skills of this verse: the target was technical brilliance, and neither originality of thought nor depth of lyrical feeling was required. Much of the verse was provided by the professional poet on demand, and praise of the leader (whether during his life or as an elegy on his death) was the theme of a good deal of it: he must be praised, too, according to certain fairly strict rules, so that we learn little that we can take as factual about the personality or appearance of the subject of any of these poems. For the production of such technically brilliant and poetically conventional verse, as well as for the benefit of their wise counsel and their learning, whole dynasties of professional poets were maintained as a powerful and respected elite by the rulers of medieval Gaelic kingdoms.

This, at any rate, is the picture painted from Irish evidence by Eleanor Knott[31] and others, but it is becoming clear that the situation in Scotland may have been a little more complex. It may yet be shown that only a small number of Scottish chiefs maintained learned poets of this kind, known in modern Gaelic as *filidhean* (singular *file* or *filidh*, in Classical Gaelic *file*). When we come to the seventeenth century we find only three principal families of these *filidhean* in Scotland: the family of Mac Muireadhaigh (in modern Gaelic *MacMhuirich*) serving the

MacDonalds of Clanranald, the family of Ó Muirgheasáin serving Sìol Tormaid (the MacLeods of Dunvegan) and probably the Macleans of Duart, and the family of Mac Eoghain serving the Campbells of Argyll. (It is important to remember, however, that poets were not necessarily limited to composing for the families they were traditionally supposed to 'serve'.) Other names of poetic families are known, and the situation before 1600 is much less well documented, but all three of the above-named families have links (or possible links) with Ireland. Some think the *file* was considerably less significant in medieval Scotland than he was in Ireland; further research will be needed before we can be sure.

Those three families are very important contributors to the literature of seventeenth-century Scotland, as representatives of the old 'high' art shared by Scotland and Ireland. In terms of theme the examples (nos VII and XVIII, both by MacMhuirich poets) which we have chosen from this learned Classical tradition are not really representative of it, for they are certainly not straightforward formal poems of praise, the principal 'commercial' output of the professional poets. However, in the matter of theme the seventeenth century itself was not one of great innovation either, and more-or-less formulaic praise of the chief continues to be a dominant theme in poems and songs of most types, both classical and vernacular. Nos IX, XVI, XIX, XXIV, XXVII, XXVIII, XXXIV, XXXV and XXXVI are songs of praise to chiefs or heroes, songs whose social function was similar to that of Classical praise poetry, namely to re-affirm the desirability of the status quo in Gaelic society.

This professional learned poetry of 1200-c.1650 is often referred to as 'bardic' poetry, but the term is not strictly accurate. These professionals were not covered by the original meaning of the Gaelic word *bard*; they would have been insulted to have been so called, for the *bard* (in Classical Gaelic, prior to the Scottish vernacular Gaelic of the seventeenth century) was a much less learned type of poet, who would probably have been viewed with contempt by the *file*, or learned poet. The English word 'bardic' is inaccurate when used to describe the work of the professional syllabic poet, or *file*; it is probably a fairly meaningless word anyway, since the word *bard* in English (if we ignore heavy Celtic and pseudo-Celtic overtones) seems to mean very little more than 'poet'. Strictly, then, a bardic poet is a tautology.

With this caveat, however, as to the propriety of its use, we will
have to accept that the term 'bardic poetry' is in common use
among critics and scholars to denote the Gaelic professional
poetry of the period 1200-c.1650.

Amateur syllabic poetry

The strict application of rules for professional syllabic verse, *dán
díreach*, was an innovation of c.1200 by the learned poetic class,
at least partially intended to ensure social acceptance and awe
of their art and power. But syllabic verse does not have to be
strict, does not have to be *dán díreach*; in our no. XVII Cathal
MacMhuirich seems to be pointing up the incompetence of a bad
poet by himself making use of 'imperfect' rhymes. This is, of
course, an exceptional case, but much of our earliest Gaelic
verse, including the remarkable nature poetry of the 9th-12th
centuries, the Ossianic lays of the 12th-16th centuries and the
romantic love poetry of the 14th-17th centuries, makes use of
syllabic metres with rhymes, alliteration and other metrical orna-
ment very much less elaborate than *dán díreach*. The same
tradition continued also in Ireland during the seventeenth cen-
tury and later,[32] and in Scotland is best represented in the Fernaig
manuscript.

The Fernaig manuscript is different from all other Gaelic
manuscripts in several ways, not least because it is the only
collection of Scottish Gaelic verse we have which was actually
committed to paper in the seventeenth century; most of the verse
of the century, as we will see, was composed without the use of
writing, and what now survives was not written down before the
eighteenth century. The Fernaig manuscript stands almost alone
in preserving for us a strand of Gaelic verse which without it we
would hardly know about, the 'amateur syllabic poetry' to be
discussed below.

Consisting of two small volumes written in a strange spelling
(based on English spelling), the manuscript was written between
1688 and 1693 by Donnchadh nam Pìos, Duncan Macrae of
Inverinate in Kintail, Wester Ross (c.1640-c.1700). Now in
Glasgow University Library, this personal anthology contains
pre-1600 as well as post-1600 verse, some of it (including no.
XXXVIII here) by Donnchadh himself, and there is a sizeable

percentage of religious verse: this in itself also marks the collection off from the generality of the surviving vernacular verse of that century, which includes virtually no religious song.

But much of the content of the Fernaig manuscript is distinguished by being in a form of syllabic verse much less strict and ornate than the Classical *dán díreach*, and the language is basically the Scottish Gaelic vernacular, though drawing freely on Classical language forms. Take as an example the 7th quatrain of no. XII, a poem of perhaps c.1630 in the manuscript; the metrical formula is basically *rannaigheacht mhór* (the strict form of which is described above):

> Is mairg a ta beò nan dèidh
> 'S a ta gun spèis fo bheil cion;
> Thug an anshocair mo leòn
> Bho nach maireann beò na fir.

Here the syllable count is fine (seven syllables per line); but the final rhyme *cion: fir* is bad in Classical terms because the vowels are not identical. While *cion* and *fir* have short vowels, *dèidh* and *leòn* have long vowels. The *aicill* between *leòn* and *beò* would be 'imperfect' to the professional poet because the *-n* in *leòn* is not matched by any consonant in *beò*. This less strict verse also likes to have *aicill* in the first couplet (*dán díreach* does not), so that we here have *dèidh* rhyming with *spèis*; but this is an 'imperfect' rhyme too, because *-dh* and *-s* belong to different consonant groups according to the Classical poets. And there is neither internal rhyme nor alliteration.

It would be easy to view poems such as this one simply as unsuccessful or incompetent attempts at 'proper' syllabic verse: after all, the poets represented in the manuscript, or most of them, were not paid as poets (as far as we know). But this might be a mistake, for we have no reason to think that the poets represented in the manuscript were attempting to compose in *dán díreach*.

This less strict syllabic poetry has been called 'semi-bardic' and 'sub-bardic', probably with the implication that it is not quite 'bardic'. But if we reject 'bardic' as a designation for Classical professional syllabic verse, then perhaps we must look for some other term for the verse which makes up the bulk of the Fernaig manuscript. No exact term suggests itself, but perhaps 'amateur syllabic poetry' will serve – even if that term might also be held to cover the *dán díreach* work of professional poets when writing in a personal capacity (as in the case of no. VII, probably).

As to the poets who composed the written verse of the seventeenth century, we can easily identify the professionals whose ideal was *dán díreach*: they were the elite hereditary class of *filidhean*, maintained by the chiefs. It is not so simple with the amateurs, but a look at the names of the authors identified in the Fernaig manuscript may allow us to confirm what we may well have expected: that the amateurs are members of the aristocracy (minor, perhaps) and the professions (including the clergy), and often of both. Thus we find there poems (nos XI–XIV) ascribed to Donnchadh MacRaoiridh, who may have been a member of an old professional poetic family not otherwise represented, as far as we know, by extant verse; minor aristocrats include MacCulloch of Park, near Dingwall, Sir Eoin Stewart of Appin, Murchadh Mòr MacKenzie of Achilty in Easter Ross (author also of the songs which are nos XXX and XXXI) and Gille Calum Garbh, chief of the MacLeods of Raasay (d. 1610); Stewart may well have been a clergyman also.

This amateur verse is not entirely confined to the Fernaig manuscript, and we have another example as no. XXXIII from an 18th-century Maclean manuscript: again the author is an aristocrat, Gilleasbaig na Ceapaich (d. 1682), 15th chief of the MacDonalds of Keppoch and a fairly productive poet in the song tradition.

Waulking songs

Unlike the syllabic verse (both strict and 'amateur') already discussed, the rest of the verse of the seventeenth century is song, not 'poetry' in the sense of something to be read. Due to all the social, political and religious upheavals of the century, and doubtless also to the end of the Gaelic education provided for the learned families of professional poets, literacy in Gaelic seems to have been a comparatively rare skill in the seventeenth century; and so it remained well into the present half-century, as the system directed all educational resources towards education in and through English. As a result, most of the song of the seventeenth century survived for a considerable time in the oral tradition only: the songs were doubtless composed without recourse to writing, and transmitted orally by singing before (and involving) various kinds of audience.

One effect of this, probably, was the exercise of a fairly rigorous mixture of practical criticism and censorship: if those who heard a song didn't like it, for any reason, they would not perform it or pass it on, so that the song would pass out of oral currency and be lost. Almost certainly a very large number of songs composed in the seventeenth century have been lost in this way, and we can only guess at what percentage the extant remainder amounts to.

The earliest song tradition we have appears to be that represented in part by the waulking songs, the only choral songs surviving in modern Gaelic tradition (they survive also in Nova Scotia, Canada, where they are called 'milling songs'). Waulking songs are choral in that they are performed in conjunction with communal labour, not that they were intended for singing by choirs of any more formal kind. To the same tradition belonged other work-songs, like the boat-song or rowing song (*iorram*) which seems to have gone out of use, as such, around the middle of the nineteenth century; but the waulking song, sung to accompany the traditional work of fulling cloth, remained as part of living tradition until the 1950s: sound and video recordings have made it possible also to stage simulated waulking sessions even more recently.[33]

Most waulking songs are not datable, but we have a number which we can with confidence date, at least partly, to the seventeenth century, and some to the sixteenth. It is impossible to say how old the tradition is, probably as old as the traditional method of fulling cloth by communal beating, almost certainly considerably older than the sixteenth century, even if we cannot date any of the extant songs so early. This raises the interesting point of the status of songs (of all kinds) in the period between 1200 and 1600, when our only direct information is about the written and (more or less) learned poetry of the upper crust. We cannot know for sure, because there is no direct evidence, but it stands to reason that the ordinary Gael must always have had a tradition of singing: it is likely that the tradition of the waulking songs was developing among women who did this work all through the pre-1600 'Classical' period, but was not written down. In fact serious and systematic writing down and recording of songs in this tradition did not really get under way until well into the twentieth century. This was over a century later than the large-scale collection of other types of songs from the oral tradition.

The most prominent and essential feature of a waulking song was probably always its regular and clear beat, which fitted the beating process of the waulking (and in the *iorram* doubtless marked the strokes of the oars). It is thus a paradox that in most cases the basic structure of the lines of verse is syllabic – the type of line-construction which seems least suitable for a regular beat. In simple terms, the singer(s) must stress syllables which would normally be unstressed, in order to keep the beat regular. Here is an example from our no. XV, where each of the lines has eight syllables:

> 'S fliuch an oidhche nochd 's gur fuar i.
> Ma thug Clann Nìll druim a' chuain orr,
> Luchd nan seòl geal 's nan long luatha
> 'S nam brataichean dearg is uaine . . .

In the first of these the beat is simple and regular, so that the line is metrically very like

> Swift of foot was Hiawatha.

But in the second line the normal Gaelic stress-system would have its main stresses on *thug, Nìll, druim* and *chuain,* giving an irregular pattern of beats, which would ruin the whole purpose of providing strict rhythm for the waulking. In the third line a regular pattern of four beats would demand a beat on *nan* (which is the article, 'the'), whereas the stress would naturally fall on *long* ('ships'). In the fourth line the 'natural' rhythm (stressing *brat-*) gives only three beats instead of four. (A similar problem of irregularity of beat would occur in English if the line quoted above had been written, with exactly the same syllables, as

> Hiawatha was swift of foot.)

In practical use, for waulking, this remarkable tension between metre and rhythm in the waulking songs is resolved by giving the

beat precedence, and over-riding the normal speech-rhythms of
the syllabic verse. But if the beat is everything, why then did the
composers of these songs persist in composing them in syllabic
metres? We have seen no answer to this question, and it is one
which arises again in relation to other seventeenth-century songs.

The related Gaelic tradition of Ireland does not have the
waulking song tradition nor, as far as we know, has anything
closely related to it survived there; for singing at work it seems
Irish workers, like workers everywhere else, would simply have
used songs of any structure, whether chosen at random or
composed for the purpose.

Perhaps it will emerge (after much further research) that in the
period 1200–1600 syllabic verse was the only, or the commonest,
type of verse available at all levels of Highland culture, whether
it was used for reading, recitation or singing, by the learned
classes or by the non-literate women who waulked the cloth.

Another distinctive feature of waulking songs is the large
numbers of meaningless vocables interspersed in the text: often
a leading singer would sing the text and all the other workers
would sing the chorus of vocables. The units of text separated by
the vocables may be single lines (nos I, IV, XXI, XXV, XXXI)
or half lines (V, VIII, XV) or couplets (II, XXIII, XXXII). Since
we have no tune for no. XXXV it is impossible to be sure how
its text was divided – or indeed if it belongs to the waulking song
class at all. It has been pointed out that the form based on
couplets seems to have been popular among poets who were not
concerned with work songs at all, and used it simply as another
metrical form.

The meaningless vocables were basically intended only for the
waulking (or rowing) process: to extend the song to fit, as far as
possible, the time needed to waulk a piece of cloth, a process
which might take three hours (or to reach the boat's destination).
Margaret Fay Shaw, who made an important collection of South
Uist waulking songs in the 1930s, comments on the fact that, in
performance, many of these songs were very long: 'With the
longest it often happens that they are a combination of two or
more songs, but one should remember that these songs must at
times be lengthened in order to fulfil their purpose, and that is
the time needed to shrink the cloth, and that verses and parts of
other songs have been added and so included with repetition

over the years.'[34] For this reason it is seldom possible to be completely sure that we have the 'original' complete text of a waulking song.

As to the poets who made these songs, we can name no certain identifiable authors, but tradition usually ascribes them (with or without names) to the women who sang them at the waulking board, basically as extempore compositions. Extempore or not, the songs draw heavily on well-known formulae, which explains why similarities of text are sometimes to be seen.

It is sometimes hard to be sure, but some of our extant waulking songs probably began life as rowing songs: in the case of our nos I and VIII, which in metrical terms we can call waulking songs, it is quite clear, both from the subject-matter and from extant tradition, that we have early instances of the *iorram*. And songs of other metrical types, especially if they have a regular beat, might also be used for either waulking or rowing. It is on record that no. XXX, which has *iorram* in its title, was used as a rowing song at least once in 1787.[35]

In the case of nos III and XXIX it is possible that we have something of an intermediate stage between the waulking song and the rest of the fully-stressed verse of the seventeenth century. In these the unit is the couplet, one of those found in waulking songs, and favoured (perhaps) by songmakers for uses other than fulling the cloth; but in these two cases there is no real evidence of a syllabic base (in other words, we clearly have a pattern of regular beats) and there are no meaningless vocables. The tune for no.III, at least, confirms that it is 'strophic'.

Strophic verse

Perhaps the most distinctive Scottish Gaelic song type to emerge as a popular form in the seventeenth century is that distinguished by three-line stanzas with a clear regular beat; examples in this collection are nos IX, X, XVI, XIX, XXVII, XXVIII, XXX and XXXIV. The term *strophic* has been used of this type probably because the three-line stanzas are not metrically complete in themselves: the final rhyming word of each stanza rhymes, not within the stanza itself, but with the final of the other stanzas of the song. Therefore each of these stanzas can be seen as a *strophe*, or component part of a notional larger stanza.

These strophic stanzas, consisting of three lines, are asymmetrical, and one way of singing them places two together, or simply repeats the stanza, so that in performance we have in effect of a (symmetrical) six-line stanza. But the basic asymmetrical nature of the stanza is confirmed when the song is (more commonly) sung with the third line repeated as a fourth.

It is probably significant that this verse-form does not occur in the related Gaelic tradition of Ireland. Our no. IX may be the earliest extant example of it, and it remained popular through the eighteenth century and later. At least two different suggestions have been made as to its origin.

It has been held that this three-line strophic song was originally a type commonly used by the true *bard* of the pre-1600 period, that is, the relatively unlearned (in comparison with the *file*) poet who may have been the most widely employed poet in Scotland, and who may not, it is assumed, have used writing for his compositions: as has been suggested above, the families of *filidhean*, apparently so numerous in Ireland, may have been fewer in Scotland. Two facts may offer some support for this idea: we appear to have evidence from tradition that Eachann Bacach (c. 1600–*post*1651), the author of several songs in this metre, including our no. XVI, was maintained as a poet by the chief of the Macleans of Duart (though we have no evidence of any other of our seventeenth-century song-makers being maintained as poets). Secondly the word for a 'poet' in modern Scottish Gaelic is *bàrd*, whereas in Irish the word is *file*; this might be held to confirm that for a considerable period the less learned poet was the best known poet in Scotland.

Those who support this view, that we have here a song tradition with regular rhythm which was in use for a long time before 1600, then point to the undoubted similarities which exist between the seventeenth-century strophic verse and various early medieval Gaelic metres, especially those known as *ochtfhoclach*, which are distinguished by groups of short lines each followed a longer line.[36]

An alternative view emphasises the regular rhythm of seventeenth-century strophic verse, and the fact that two or four stanzas (*strophes*) can be combined to give a verse-form perfectly normal and widespread in much of Western European song. A stanza in three-line strophic verse can be viewed as metrically close to a strophe like

> Near Banbridge town
> In the County Down
> One morning in last July . . .

Four of these combine to make a normal 12-line stanza (usually written in eight lines); a good instance of such a stanza is that of the poem *An Cill Dubhaich mo thàmh cha laigh dhomh sàmh* in the Fernaig manuscript. In this view, then, the three-line strophic metre may be a relatively recent import into the Scottish Gaelic tradition, introduced (along with other song-types yet to be discussed here) as part of a general package of clearly-stressed song types, but then somehow developing as a distinct form – as most imports into Gaelic metrics tend to do.

Obviously it will never be possible to be quite sure which, if either, of these views most closely reflects historical fact in regard to the metre of such songs. It may be relevant that some poems in this three-line metre (such as nos XVI and XXX here) have the word *iorram* in the titles they are given in the written or printed eighteenth-century sources. Speculation has therefore arisen (and been rejected) that this metre is also somehow essentially linked to boat-songs, but we do not yet know nearly enough about the three-line strophic metre to allow us to say anything with confidence about its origin and history.

Whatever its origin, the three-line strophic metre was adapted during the seventeenth century into a new and remarkable form in which the number of lines could vary from stanza to stanza. Màiri nighean Alasdair Ruaidh and Eachann Bacach composed songs in this form, and it has been held that Eachann Bacach invented it, in a song on the death of Sir Lachlann of Duart in 1649. Our example, however, is no. XXIV, which is possibly a little older. Whether no. XXXVI is yet another example of this 'irregular strophic' metre is open to question. The poet there may have been seeking to use a (?new) nine-line strophic form, in which case he failed (or the scribe of the only extant version has made a mistake), for the fifth stanza has only eight lines. Alternatively the song may have been composed in 'irregular strophic' metre and the number of lines turned out to be eight or nine 'by accident'.

No. VI also appears to have a kind of strophic metre, but in the absence of a tune we cannot be sure: it is possible that in performance the chorus was sung together with each stanza to form a perfectly normal symmetrical verse. Much the same may apply to no. XXVI, though in that case we have neither tune nor chorus.

Other types of song

If strophic verse is a distinctive type of Scottish Gaelic song, we have no reason to claim, at least in a seventeenth-century context, that it was the preserve of any kind of specialist 'strophic poets'. On the contrary, it is one of a range of song types which any composer of songs might draw on. We have examples of its use in the works of practically all the known song-makers of the century, but they always use other forms as well.

One interesting type is what we may call the 'syllabic song', a song whose words, like those of the waulking song, were composed in a syllabic metre (or, perhaps more accurately, survive for us in a form which appears to be of syllabic structure). Our no. XX is an excellent example, with eight syllables per line and a tune which, like those of the waulking songs, might be seen as over-riding the demand of the text for speech-stress and imposing a rhythm which is (nearly) regular. No. XLIII is very similar. The question as to whether a particular song is basically of this type or not can still cause disagreement: was the text composed to a (more-or-less strict) syllabic pattern, or was it composed to fit extant tunes which demand, or seem to demand, regular rhythmical beats? Our no. XLII is, I think, a good example of this conflict, which the reader can solve for himself. Even if the text of no. XLII has eight syllables per line, it will still not fit the regularity of rhythm demanded by the 'Hiawatha' line noted above. But the solution may be that suggested by the Reverend William Matheson[37]: that we think, not of metre and tune as two different things, but of a single 'complex of words and music' which can, where necessary, involve syncopated types of rhythm, as well as the enforced regularisation of an irregular metrical line by a strong musical beat.

Another popular verse-form for seventeenth-century song is the stanza which consists basically of four five-stress lines: principally because printed pages are fairly narrow, these stanzas are generally written as eight lines, the first line of each couplet having two stresses and the second three. Nos. XL and XLI are good examples, and it will be seen that internal rhyme (which may look like *aicill* when the stanza is written in eight lines) is a prominent feature of this verse-form. This metrical form seems to have surfaced in Ireland before 1600, but there is no need to assume that its occurrence here is due to borrowing from Ireland.

Similarly we have four-stress lines, with internal rhyme, as in no. XXXVII; and there is a variety of other song types, of which we have instances at nos VI, XXII and XXXIX. It seems fairly clear that most poets in the seventeenth century had a wide range of metres/tune types to choose from freely, for their products may include any selection from the various song-types here referred to, including strophic verse and 'syllabic song', as well as waulking song structures. But it is also clear that these 'song-poets' were not limited even to the narrow range of song forms: as we have seen, Murchadh Mòr, as well as composing nos XXX (in strophic metre) and XXXI, also contributed 'amateur syllabic' poetry to the Fernaig manuscript; and Niall MacMhuirich (d.1726), the last of the professional syllabic poets in his family, is well known for two laments he made in 1715 in strophic metres.

And if, as has been pointed out above, many of the 'amateur syllabic' poets (including Murchadh Mòr, Gilleasbaig na Ceapaich and Donnchadh nam Pìos) belonged to the aristocracy, it is also notable that a considerable number of the main named song-makers of the seventeenth century were also related to the chiefs. Iain Lom belonged to *Sliochd a' bhràthar bu shine* ('the descendants of the eldest brother'), a branch of the Keppoch MacDonalds which claimed seniority over the ruling Keppoch family. Màiri nighean Alasdair Ruaidh was within a few generations of the ruling family of Sìol Tormaid, and An Clàrsair Dall was in the direct line of *Sliochd a' Bhritheimh* ('the descendants of the judge'), the Morrison judges of Ness in Lewis. An Ciaran Mabach was a brother of the chief of the MacDonalds of Sleat.

Sources

In general the Gaelic song of the seventeenth century, and long afterwards, was the only literature the people had, their only political and social comment, and so its central concern with bolstering a threatened social order is not surprising. Usually this is done by praising chiefs and leaders, according to a broadly fixed formula or 'code' (well illustrated in no. XIX)[38]: when a chief is praised the poet *must* praise his generosity, his noble ancestry, his skill in hunting, and a range of other praiseworthy 'good points'. Not surprisingly, this can lead to a degree of similarity between songs praising chiefs who may, in fact, have had quite disparate ranges of 'good points'. Occasionally the poet finds it necessary to criticise a chief's behaviour, as in no. XLI, and perhaps in no. XVI. But whatever kind of song is being made, there is none of the modern literateur's need always to be saying something new, for the basic message must remain the same. The poetry is in general not lyrical, for the personal feelings of the poet, or of anyone else, are of little interest to his/her audience. The Gaelic poet in those days was a representative of his/her class, not of any super-sensitive minority.

As we have seen, the Fernaig manuscript seems to be the only collection of vernacular Scottish Gaelic verse actually written in the seventeenth century. For the rest of the verse we are forced to rely, almost entirely, on later collectors, many of them clergymen of the Established Church, who noted the songs (in most cases the words only) from oral performance in the period following the disaster of Culloden in 1746. Some of the collections are printed, others remain in manuscript. The following are among the most important:

MS collections:

The collection of the Reverend James **MacLagan** (1728–1805), minister of Blair Atholl, Perthshire; now in Glasgow University Library.

The collection of the Reverend Donald **MacNicol** (1735–1802), minister of Lismore and Appin, Argyllshire; part of the collection is in the National Library, another part in private hands but on deposit in Edinburgh University Library.

The collection (in a single volume dated 1770), of Eoghan **Macdhiarmid** (d.1801), who was to become minister of Comrie in Perthshire; now in Glasgow University Department of Celtic, this has recently been published in part by Derick S. Thomson, *The Macdiarmid MS Anthology* (1992); another volume (volume I, 1769) is known to have existed but is now lost.

The volume written by Dr **Hector Maclean** (1704–c.1785) of Gruline in Mull, between 1738 and 1768; now in the Public Archives of Nova Scotia, Halifax.

Printed collections:

The Eigg Collection: Raonuill Macdomhnuill Ann 'N Eilean Eigg, *Co-chruinneachidh orannaigh Gaidhealach,* vol. I, Duneidiunn: Ruddiman, 1776.

Gillies' Collection: *A collection of ancient and modern Gaelic poems and songs, transmitted from gentlemen in the Highlands of Scotland to the editor,* Perth: John Gillies, 1786.

The **Stewarts' Collection:** Alexander and Donald Stewart, A.M., *Cochruinneacha taoghta de shaothair nam bard Gaëleach,* Duneidin: Stiuart, 1804.

Turner's Collection: Paruig Mac-an-Tuairneir, *Comh-chruinneacha do dh' orain taghta, Ghaidhealach,* Duneidionn: Stiubhard, 1813.

Clearly some of our seventeenth-century songs are available to us only in texts written down more than a hundred years (sometimes much more) after their composition. Having been composed in the oral tradition, they spent the intervening period (or most of it) in the oral tradition and it is usually impossible to be sure how close a surviving text is to what the song-maker originally composed. Editorial decisions as to text are therefore always open to question. And where a tune for a song has survived, still attached to it, till the present day, or at least long enough to be written down, the fact still remains that we rarely have clear positive evidence as to what tune the poet originally had in mind. The texts and tunes of songs here given are therefore not by any means definitive, and remain wide open to doubt.

The selection made here might indeed be more representative if it contained even more praise poetry, but it might then be less interesting. And it seems fair to include poems and songs which do express personal feelings, however modestly and superficially, and however unrepresentative such songs may be. Nos VII, XXX and XXXVII give vivid expression to the poets' delight in drinking, seafaring and hunting (contrasted in two cases with the dullness of real life). No. XXXI, on a literal reading, also contrasts the real delights of seafaring with the horrors of trying to sail an inferior vessel. These are real personal poems, but their sentiments were clearly shared by their audience and they do not raise any fundamental social questions, as a modern poet might feel constrained to do; a seventeenth-century poet would never think of using poetry to question the accepted views of his society.

As has been suggested, most of the songs have survived for us basically because enough people liked them enough to sing them and pass them on to others. Why so much praise and political poetry should have survived in this way is hard to explain, especially when we realise that from these songs we do not really learn anything about the persons praised, because they had to be praised according to a formula. It seems to us that Professor Donald MacAulay put his finger on the answer, in the Introduction to his anthology *Nua-Bhàrdachd Ghàidhlig* (1976, p.46):

> . . . Gaelic traditional poetry was in the main one
> of celebration and participation. The poet
> produced an artefact which enabled his audience
> to participate in their culture; to act out
> culturally reinforcing roles. The poetry was
> largely oral-based; much of it was meant to be
> sung. In such circumstances innovation was not at
> a very high premium. The verse had to make an
> immediate impact, and skill in versification and
> verbal wit culminating in the well-wrought,
> memorable phrase was therefore the basic
> requirement . . .

For listeners in a heroic society there could hardly be, even in songs of formulaic praise, many better-wrought, more memorable phrases than those in the opening lines of no. XIX:

> *A Dhòmhnaill an Dùin*
> *Mhic Ghilleasbaig nan tùr,*
> *Chaidh t'eineach 's do chliù far chàch.*

Notes

1. Ian Grimble, *Scottish islands*, London: BBC, 1988, p. 57.
2. I.F. Grant, *The Macleods: the history of a clan, 1200–1956*, London: Faber & Faber, 1959, pp.188–223; Alexander Mackenzie, *History of the Macleods*, Inverness: A. & W. Mackenzie, 1889, pp.294–339.
3. Amelia G.M. MacGregor, *History of the Clan Gregor*, vol.I, Edinburgh: Brown, 1898, pp.149–157. On the effective restoration of the surname to legality see vol. II (1901), pp.454–455.
4. A. and A. Macdonald, *The Clan Donald*, vol. II, Inverness: Northern Counties Publishing Company, 1900, pp.576–600; A. McKerral, *Kintyre in the seventeenth century*, Edinburgh: Oliver & Boyd, 1948, pp.14–22; Ronald Black, 'Colla Ciotach' (1973), *Transactions of the Gaelic Society of Inverness* [TGSI], vol. XLVIII, pp.201–215.
5. *The Clan Donald*, II, pp.406–410; *The Celtic Monthly*, vol. IX (1901), pp.32–33.
6. *The Clan Donald*, III (1904), pp.38–46.
7. Gordon Donaldson, *Scottish historical documents*, New York: Barnes & Noble, 1970, pp.174–175. On the Statutes in general see Grant, *Macleods*, pp.208–223.
8. David Stevenson, *Alasdair MacColla and the Highland problem in the seventeenth century*, Edinburgh: Donald, 1980, pp.28–30.
9. Philip S. Robinson, *The plantation of Ulster*, Dublin: Gill & Macmillan, 1984, pp.9–128; J.C. Beckett, *The making of modern Ireland, 1603–1923*, London: Faber & Faber, 1966, pp. 21–48.
10. Stevenson, *Alasdair MacColla*, pp.62–64.
11. R.L. Thomson (ed.), *Foirm na n-urrnuidheadh: John Carswell's Gaelic translation of the Book of Common Order*, Edinburgh: Scottish Gaelic Texts Society [SGTS], 1970; ibid., *Adtimchiol an chreidimh: the Gaelic version of John Calvin's Catechismus Ecclesiae Genevensis*, SGTS, 1962.
12. Ronald I.M. Black, 'The Gaelic manuscripts of Scotland', *Gaelic and Scotland: Alba agus a' Ghàidhlig* (ed. W. Gillies), Edinburgh University Press, 1989, pp. 151–160.
13. in John Dwyer, R.A. Mason and A. Murdoch, *New perspectives on the politics and culture of early modern Scotland*, Edinburgh: Donald, [1982], p.69.
14. Alexander Cameron, *Reliquiae Celticae*, vol. II, Inverness: Northern Counties Publishing Company, 1894, p. 182; Stevenson, *Alasdair MacColla*, pp.145–150.
15. Stevenson, *Alasdair MacColla*, pp.95–211; Edward J. Cowan, *Montrose: for covenant and king*, London: Weidenfeld and Nicolson, 1977, pp.130–251; David Stevenson, *The Covenanters: the National Covenant and Scotland*, Edinburgh: Saltire Society, 1988, pp.1–54.
16. Edward J. Cowan, 'Montrose and Argyll', *The Scottish nation* (ed. Gordon Menzies), London: BBC, 1972, pp.118–132; Stevenson, *Alasdair MacColla*, pp.213–264; Black, 'Colla Ciotach', pp.227–231; George Hill, *An historical account of the Macdonnells of Antrim*,

Belfast: Archer, 1873, pp.101–114; Angus Matheson, 'Traditions of Alasdair mac Colla', *Transactions of the Gaelic Society of Glasgow*, vol.V (1958), p.90, n.10; John Mackechnie, *Catalogue of Gaelic manuscripts in selected libraries in Great Britain and Ireland*, vol.I, Boston: Hall, 1973, p.468.

17. Allan Macinnes, 'The first Scottish Tories?', *Scottish Historical Review*, vol. LXVII (1988), pp.56–66; David Stevenson, *Revolution and counter-revolution in Scotland 1644–1651*, London: Royal Historical Society, 1977, pp.82–122.

18. Cowan, 'Montrose and Argyll', pp.128–130; Cowan, *Montrose*, pp.276–301.

19. A. Maclean Sinclair, *The Clan Gillean*, Charlottetown P.E.I.: Haszard and Moore, 1899, pp.193–196.

20. Grant, *Macleods*, pp.292–297.

21. *The Clan Donald*, II, pp.427–438.

22. R.L. Thomson, 'The language of the Shorter Catechism (1659)', *Scottish Gaelic Studies* [SGS], vol. XII, part I (1971), pp.34-51; ibid., 'The language of the Caogad', SGS, vol. XII, part II (1976), pp.143–182.

23. Annie M. Mackenzie, *Orain Iain Luim*, SGTS, 1964, pp.268–286; Mackechnie, *Catalogue*, vol. I, pp.420–421.

24. Maclean Sinclair, *The Clan Gillean*, pp.178–225; J.L. Campbell and Derick Thomson, *Edward Lhuyd in the Scottish Highlands, 1699–1700*, Oxford: Clarendon, 1963, pp. 18–21.

25. Stevenson, *Covenanters*, pp.59–69; John R. Elder, *The Highland host of 1678*, Glasgow: MacLehose, 1914.

26. Donald Maclean, *Typographia Scoto-Gadelica*, Edinburgh: Grant, 1915, p.318; Duncan C. Mactavish, *The Gaelic psalms, 1694*, Lochgilphead: Annan, 1934, pp.xii–xiii.

27. C. Sanford Terry, *John Graham of Claverhouse, Viscount of Dundee*, London: Constable, 1905, pp.319–345; Stuart Reid, *Killiecrankie 1689*, Leigh-on-sea: Partisan Press, 1989; Paul Hopkins, *Glencoe and the end of the Highland war*, Edinburgh: Donald, 1986, pp.150–161.

28. Victor E. Durkacz, *The decline of the Celtic languages*, Edinburgh: Donald, 1983, pp. 17–22; Charles W.J. Withers, *Gaelic in Scotland 1698–1981*, Edinburgh: Donald, 1984, p.43.

29. Hopkins, *Glencoe*; John Prebble, *Glencoe: the story of the massacre*, Penguin, 1968.

30. Derick Thomson, 'The seventeenth-century crucible of Scottish Gaelic poetry', *Studia Celtica*, vol. XXVI–XXVII (1991–92), pp.155–162.

31. Eleanor Knott, *The bardic poems of Tadhg Dall O Huiginn (1550–1591)*, vol. I, London: Irish Texts Society, 1922, pp.xxxiii–xlv; Derick Thomson, *An introduction to Gaelic poetry*, Edinburgh University Press, 1990, pp.19–56.

32. Brian Ó Cuív, 'Some developments in Irish metrics', *Éigse*, vol. XII, pp.273–290.

33. For detailed discussion of the waulking process see J.L. Campbell and Francis Collinson, *Hebridean folksongs*, vol. I, Oxford: Clarendon,

1969, pp.3–16; *idem*, vol. III (1981), pp.2–5.

34. Margaret Fay Shaw, *Folksongs and folklore of South Uist*, Oxford University Press, 1977, p.74. See also *Celtica*, vol. XV (1983), pp. 182–183.
35. see C. Ó Baoill, *Eachann Bacach and other Maclean poets*, SGTS, 1979, p.279; see also Francis Collinson, *The traditional and national music of Scotland*, London: Routledge and Kegan Paul, 1966, pp.78–81.
36. John MacInnes, 'Gaelic songs of Mary Macleod', SGS, vol. XI (1966), pp.20–23; William Matheson, *The Blind Harper*, SGTS, 1970, pp. 149–152; Derick S. Thomson, 'The poetic tradition in Gaelic Scotland', *Proceedings of the seventh international conference of Celtic studies* (ed. D. Ellis Evans, J.G. Griffith and E.M. Jope), Oxford, 1986, pp.124–127. On the *ochtfhoclach* metres see Gerard Murphy, *Early Irish metrics*, Dublin: Royal Irish Academy, 1961, pp.70–73.
37. SGS, vol. XIV, part I (1983), p.132.
38. see John MacInnes, 'The panegyric code in Gaelic poetry and its historical background' (1978), TGSI, vol. L, pp.435–498.

Translator's Note

Translating is largely a matter of making compromises. While it may theoretically be possible for a translation to be an improvement on the original, it often seems that much of what makes a work attractive in the first place is in danger of being lost in translation. Different translators, depending on the purpose of their translations, will conceive of different principles to guide them through this painful process. If the reader is to be able to draw conclusions with any confidence about the nature of the original literature, it seems essential to explain in each case what these guiding principles are.

My aims in producing the translations in this book have been two-fold, and to some extent, conflicting. Firstly they are intended to provide a useful crib for the limited reader of Gaelic. To this end the translations are fairly literal: rather than being a creative reworking of the content of entire poems, these translations represent the originals word by word and line by line. For the same reason the Gaelic verb forms and idioms are retained even where these are not normal in English. (Perhaps there is no harm, in any case, in allowing a translation to surprise the reader with the ways another language may view the world.)

It could be argued that the needs of the reader with limited Gaelic would be better served by a literal translation in prose, but my second set of aims concerns the reader with no Gaelic. There is something so simple about the notion that poetry in one language is best translated into another also as poetry that it may even be true. Poetry may demand a relaxation of syntax and an arrangement of thought and image which, if translated into prose, could look so odd as to be a misrepresentation of the original. This is my chief defence for translating poetry as poetry, whatever the frustrations. Prose raises a different set of expectations.

These frustrations are well-rehearsed in every translator's note. Of all the different aspects of poetry – meaning, rhythm, rhyme, and other ornamentation, the texture of the language in general, the collocations and register of individual words – what can be sacrificed, and in what order should these sacrifices be made? Doubtless there are many valid orders; all I can do is explain my own.

To the accurate representation of meaning (as far as I understand it) I have given first place. Second place I have given to an attempt to mimic the rhythm of the originals, in particular the number of stresses per line and the stress pattern at the end of lines, where the final beat may fall on the last, second or third last syllable. It should be remembered that the stress does not always fall on the first syllable of a word in English, unlike the case, generally, in Gaelic. The translations then may not actually *look* to be following the stress patterns of the originals. I have made no attempt to mimic those metres based on syllable- rather than stress-count as such metres generally make little sense in stress-timed languages. Suffice it to say in this regard that, in the waulking songs in particular, the reader should be prepared to stress a syllable, possibly a conjunction or preposition, not normally stressed in English (or in Gaelic) for the sake of keeping the beat regular.

Apart from the retention of rhythm, I have retained very little other ornamentation, which, as explained in the introduction, could be enormously exacting. Of all the different forms rhyme could take – internal, end, *aicill*, both perfect and imperfect – I have only made an attempt at end rhyme, representing it crudely as assonance, and that only occasionally (for example in nos. VII, XIV, XXIV, XXVII, XXX). Otherwise the wealth of mandatory ornamentation, a source of such great pride to the professional poet and cognoscenti, is sadly lost on my English reader.

Inseparable from the dictionary meaning of words is the less definable atmosphere they carry with them. It is striking in the Gaelic poetry of this period how central and simple the vocabulary is, imparting a kind of understated dignity and uniformity to the poetry as a whole. Seldom do we feel the poet has taken a delight in coming up with a surprising adjective or unexpected verb. In diction then, as well as in subject-matter, this is clearly a conventionalised poetry, and in translating it I have tried to reflect the ordinariness of its vocabulary.

Some things can be translated, others cannot, and some are perhaps best left untranslated. This I feel is the case with personal names and some place-names where the Gaelic-ness of the name would seem to be part of its essential quality. I fear my earlier claim to have translated poetry into poetry is an oversimplification. The very appearance of most of these poems in writing is in itself a spurious 'translation' of the medium of song. It need hardly be said that singing produces a very different aesthetic from speech, let alone from reading. Whether or not lines are repeated, as they often are in the performance of these songs, their delivery in song is much slower than in speech, so images linger longer in the mind, as do ornaments in the ear. This makes for a mounting tension which is drastically, if not entirely, reduced on the printed page.

In concluding, I would like to express my debt in arriving at these translations to those who have edited the originals and may have translated them before, and to the editor of the present volume for many improvements. I hope that all sorts of readers may feel that, despite the compromises, something of worth is retained.

MEG BATEMAN

Note on the Tunes

Since the case is made in the Introduction for seeing most of the Gaelic verse of the seventeenth century as song, rather than mere poetry, we have provided the tunes for as many of the songs as possible, 22 in all. Poems in the old syllabic metres (nos VII, XII–XIV, XVII, XVIII, XXXIII and XXXVIII) have no tunes, since they were not composed to be sung. And for a good few of the songs too I have failed to find tunes.

On the other hand, for some songs I had a choice of several tunes and in such cases, as in the selection of the texts themselves for the anthology, I simply chose the tunes I liked best. The sources of the tunes are identified in the Notes, and they include manuscript sources, printed sources and oral sources (songs sung on cassette or disc). Where tunes are transcribed from modern printed sources (as for nos I and VIII), they can be regarded as reliable; but in some cases (as nos XXVII and XXVIII) it has been felt necessary to emend the tunes as they appear in manuscript or print, and the emendations are open to question. When transcribing from sound recordings I have found considerable simplification unavoidable, and the processes followed in simplification are also open to question.

On the whole, I hope I have provided acceptable tunes for those songs for which tunes survive. If the tunes are sometimes too simple, it should be remembered that written music, as far as traditional song is concerned, can be no more than a general guide. Those familiar with the Gaelic tradition of singing will be able to sing many of the songs properly, more or less freely and ornately, even if given only the skeleton of a basic tune. But even they, as well as newcomers to Gaelic song, should at least go back to our sources (identified in the Notes) before setting out to perform the songs; for I give the tunes mainly as a guide, and as a reminder to the reader that (in the majority of cases) the art we are concerned with in this anthology is not that of poetry, but song-making.

COLM Ó BAOILL

I. Iomair Thusa, Choinnich Cridhe

This song (or perhaps only the first seven lines of it) is thought to date from around the turn of the seventeenth century, and is said to have been composed and sung by Ailean Mòr (or Ailean Britheamh), chief of the family of Mac Gille Mhoire, or Morrison, the hereditary lawyers of Lewis. The family are believed to have taken sides in the dispute concerning the succession of the MacLeods of Lewis, and to have been partly responsible for the death of Torcall Dubh, one of the claimants, in 1597. As a result, Torcall Dubh's half-brother, Niall Odhar, is here in pursuit, by boat, of Mac Gille Mhoire, who urges his boatman, Coinneach, to row hard to escape. The song is still known traditionally in Lewis, as an iorram, *or boat song.*

Iomair thusa, Choinnich cridhe,
    Nèill a mhic sna hu o rò,
Gaol nam ban òg 's gràdh nan nighean,
    Nèill a mhic sna hu o rò,
    Hò rò o hù ò.
Tha eagal mòr air mo chridhe
Gu bheil birlinn Nèill a' tighinn,
No sgoth chaol mhic Thormaid oighre.
Iomraidh mise fear ma dhithis
'S nam b'èiginn domh fear ma thriar.

Ach 's truagh nach robh mi fhèin 's Niall Odhar
An slagan beag os cionn Dhùn Odhail,
Biodag am làimh 's esan fodham:
Dhearbhainn fhèin gun rach' i domhain
'S gum biodh fuil a chinn mu ghobhal,
'S gun dèanteadh feòil 's gun dèanteadh sitheann
'S gum biodh biadh fo ghob an fhithich.
Cha d'rinn mi fhathast beud no pudhar
Mura leag mi fiadh fo bhruthach,
No biast mhaol an caolas cumhang
No dubh-sgarbh an cois na tuinne.
Chì mi 'n rudha is slagan beag eile
Anns an do mhilleadh mo chàirdean.
'S truagh nach robh mi an Ròna romham:
Cha tàinig mi riamh an cuan so roimhe

I. Row hard, Coinneach, my heart's dear

lom - air   thus-a,   Choinn-ich   cridh-e,   Nèill   a   mhic   sna   hu   o   rò,

Gaol nam ban òg's gràdh nan nigh-ean,   Nèill a   mhic sna hu o   rò,   Hò rò   o   hù ò.

Row hard, Coinneach, my heart's dear,
love of the young girls, darling of women:
my heart is in great fear that
Niall's galley is approaching
or the slim skiff of the son of heir Tormod.
I will have two row together,
if I must, then three together.

A pity I were not with Niall Odhar
in a small hollow above Dùn Odhail,
a dagger in my hand and him beneath me:
I'd show it could go in deeply,
the blood of his head about his bollocks,
there would be made venison and red meat
with food under the beak of the raven.
Not yet have I done harm or mischief,
unless to fell a deer on a hill-side
or an otter in slender narrows
or a shag at the shoreline.
I see the headland and another small hollow
where my people were wasted.
Sad I were not over there in Rona:
I never came this way on the ocean

Gun taod oirre, gun taod cluaise,
Cupaill ann am bòrd an fhuaraidh,
'S fiùran dìreach sheasadh suas innt
'S cranna fada rachadh mun cuairt air.

II. A Mhic Iain Mhic Sheumais

*The battle of Carinish in North Uist, in 1601, was part of a feud
between the MacLeods of Harris and Dunvegan (Sìol Tormaid) and
the MacDonalds of Sleat, whose lands included North Uist. The
victorious MacDonalds were led by Dòmhnall mac Iain mhic
Sheumais (who was still alive in 1656), said to have been brought up
by his foster-mother, Nic Còiseam, in Eriskay. He was wounded at
the battle, and one of many traditions says that the song (a waulking
song) was composed extempore by Nic Còiseam and a company of
women, as she pulled the arrow(s) from his body.* Blàr a' Chèithe *and*
Blàr na Feitheadh (*couplets 5–6*) *are both probably alternative
designations of the battle itself.*

A mhic Iain mhic Sheumais,
Tha do sgeul air m'aire.
  air farail ail ò
  air farail ail ò
Gruaidh ruiteach na fèileachd
Mar èibhil ga garadh.
  hi ò hi rì ho gì èileadh
  è ho hao rì i bhò
  rò ho ì o chall èile
  bhò hi rì ò ho gì ò ho

On latha thug thu an cuan ort
Laigh gruaim air na beannaibh.

Laigh smal air na speuran,
Dh'fhàs na reultan salach.

Latha Blàr a' Chèithe
Bha feum air mo leanabh.

without tackle on board, without a halyard,
shrouds at the side to windward,
a young man who would stand in her upright
and tall masts that could go round him.

II. Son of Iain, son of Seumas

Son of Iain, son of Seumas,
news of you weighs heavy,

Flushed cheek of bounty,
hot like a live coal.

Since the day you took to the ocean
darkness has lain on the mountains.

The skies look gloomy,
the stars have grown murky.

The day of the Battle of the Cèith
my nursling was needed.

Latha Blàr na Fèitheadh
Bha do lèine na ballan.

Bha an t-saighead na spreòd
Throimh chorp seòlta na glaineadh.

Bha fuil do chuim chùbhraidh
A' drùdhadh throimh'n anart.

Bha fuil do chuirp uasail
Air uachdar gach fearainn.

Bha mise ga sùghadh
Gus na thùch air m'anail.

Cuma nach do ghabh thu am bristeadh
Latha ligeadh na faladh?

Nam biodh agam curach
Gun cuirinn air chuan i,

Feuch am faighinn naidheachd
No brath an duine uasail,

No am faighinn beachd sgeula
Air ogha Sheumais a' chruadail,

A chuir iad ann an crìochaibh
Eadar Niall is Sìol Ailein.

'S nam biodh agam dorsair
Gum fosglainn a-mach thu,

No gille math iuchrach
A thruiseadh na glasaibh.

The day of the Battle of the Runnel
your shirt was blotted.

The arrow stuck out of
the skilled body of whiteness.

The blood of your sweet bosom
was soaking through the linen.

The blood of your noble body
on the surface of the country.

I drank it
till my breath was choking.

How were you not broken
on the day of the blood-letting?

If I had a coracle
I'd put it on the ocean,

To try and get tidings
or word of the noble,

to hear some rumour
of the grandson of hardy Seumas,

whom they buried in the borders
between Niall and Sìol Ailein.

And if I had a doorman,
I would bring you into the open,

Or a good lad with keys in bunches
who could rip off the fetters.

III. MacGriogair à Ruaro

One of a group of songs related to the persecution of the MacGregors by the Campbells of Breadalbane before and after 1600, which led to the outlawing of all MacGregors. Accounts of the song, traditional and otherwise, usually assume that the composer is a woman, a relative of the subject. In this version there is very little to help identify the subject, but other versions mention MacGriogair à Ruaro (in Glenlyon, Perthshire), whence the title used here. Without much real evidence the song has been dated to the early part of the seventeenth century. Any traditional tales which might have helped explain the background further have been lost, but the verses convey, in Derick Thomson's words, 'the sense of movement, action and uneasiness of the times.'

Tha mulad, tha mulad,
Gu bheil mulad gam lìonadh,

Tha mulad bochd truagh orm
'S nach dual domh dheth dìreadh.

Ged a bhuail e mi, am balach,
Gam ghearan cha bhì mi.

Ged a dhèan iad orm eucoir,
A Mhic Dè, ciod e nì mi?

Tha mo chomhaltan gaolach
'N leaba chaoil 's an cinn ìseal,

Ann an lèinteig chaoil anairt
'S i gun bhanna gun sìde oirr,

Is nach d'iarr sibh ga fuaghladh
Mnathaibh uaisle na tìre.

B'ann diubh Pàra is Maol Caluim
'S Rìgh gum b'fhearail nan dìs iad,

Agus Griogair òg ruadh ann,
D'am bu dual bhith 'n Glinn Lìobhainn,

III. MacGriogair of Roro

Sorrow, sorrow,
sorrow fills me,

Wretched poor sorrow
I cannot hope to get over.

Though he hit me, the fellow,
I won't start complaining.

Though they do me an injustice,
what can I do, O Son of the Father?

My beloved fosterbrothers
in a strait bed, their heads hidden,

In a shroud of thin linen
with no ribbons or satin,

Since you did not ask them to sew it,
the noble-women of the country.

Of them were Pàra and Maol Caluim,
Lord, a pair that were mighty.

There was young red-haired Griogair
whose right was to Glen Lyon,

D'am bu shuaicheantas giuthas
Ri bruthach ga dìreadh.

Cranna caoin air dheagh locradh
'S ite dhosach an fhìreoin,

Crann caol air dheagh shnaidheadh –
'S cuid de dh'aighear mhic rìgh e,

'S e bhith 'n làmhan Mhic Mhuirich
Ga chunbhail rèidh dìreach.

'S iad mo ghràdh na cuirp bhòidheach
Bha air a' mhòintich nan sìneadh.

'S truagh, a Rìgh, nach mi thàinig
Mar a b'àill leam san tìm ud,

Agus buidheann dhen t-seòrsa
Chaidh òg throimh na crìochan.

Nàile, bheirinn ort comhairle
Nan gabhadh tu dhìom i:

Nuair a thèid thu an taigh òsdadh
Na òl ann ach aon deoch.

Gabh do dhrama nad sheasamh
'S bi freasdlach air do dhaoine.

Na dèan diùbha da shoitheach,
Gabh an lodar no an taoman.

Paidhir dhag a bhios gleusd ort
Agus biodag gheur aotrom.

Dèan foghar den gheamhradh
'S dèan samhradh da fhaoilteach.

Whose emblem was a pine tree
rising up from a hillside.

Smooth shafts well finished,
set with the eagle's fine plumage.

A narrow shaft well whittled –
part of a prince's pleasure,

Held in MacMhuirich's hands,
keeping it straight and steady.

My love those fair bodies
stretched out on the moorland.

Oh God, it is wretched
I did not come when intended,

While that sort of party
went early through the borders.

Nàile, I could give you counsel
if from me you would take it:

When you go to a hostel
take one drink only.

Take your dram standing,
be watchful of your people.

On no dish cast aspersions,
take the ladle or the baler.

A pair of pistols become you
and a light sharp dagger.

Make autumn of winter,
of early spring make summer.

Biodh do leaba sna cragaibh
'S na caidil ach aotrom.

Ge ainmig an fheòrag
Gheibhear dòigh air a faotainn.

Ge uasal an seabhag
'S tric a ghleidhear le foill e.

IV. Ailean Dubh à Lòchaidh

Ailean Dubh mac Raghnaill, MacDonald of Lundy near Invergarry, in Lochaber, pursued the feud of his kinsman, MacDonald of Glengarry, against the MacKenzies in 1603 by a raid on Cille Chrìosd (Tarradale) in Easter Ross. A number of MacKenzies were indeed killed, but tradition has built Ailean Dubh up into something of a mass-murderer: he is said to have burned the church with its entire congregation. This song is assumed to have been sung by a MacKenzie woman.

'S toigh leam Ailean Dubh à Lòchaidh,
Mo ghaol Ailean donn a' chòta,
'S toigh leam Ailean Dubh à Lòchaidh.

Ailein, Ailein, 's ait leam beò thu.
Sguab thu mo sprèidh bhàrr na mòintich,
Loisg thu m'iodhlann chorca is eòrna,
Mharbh thu mo thriùir bhràithrean òga,
Mharbh thu m'athair is m'fhear pòsta.
'S ged rinn thu siud 's ait leam beò thu.

V. An Spaidearachd Bharrach

This waulking song is a verbal contest, similar in some ways to the 'flyting' in Lowland verse; such songs are not uncommon in Gaelic, and in this case the contest is between a South Uist woman and a Barra woman, arguing about the excellence of the ruling families of their

Let your bed be in the rock clefts
and sleep but lightly.

Though rare the squirrel
a way is found to catch it.

Though the hawk is noble
often is it held through falsehood.

IV. Ailean Dubh from Lochy

'S toigh leam Ail-ean   Dubh à   Lòch-aidh, Mo ghaol Ail-ean donn a'   chòt-a,

'S toigh leam Ail-ean   Dubh à   Lòch-aidh,   Ail-ein,   Ail-ein,   's ait leam beò thu.

I like Ailean Dubh from Lochy,
I love brown Ailean of the trim coat,
I like Ailean Dubh from Lochy.

Ailean, Ailean, I'm pleased you're living.
You swept my cattle from the moorland,
you burnt my stackyard of oats and barley,
you killed my three youthful brothers,
you killed my father and my husband.
Though you did that, I'm pleased you're living.

V. The Barra Boasting

Fa liù   o ho,   A Dhia! is gaol-ach Fa liù   o ho,   lium an   gill-e,
                                                                    Fine

O hao   ri   o ho,   Hi o ho hao o ho   Fa liù   o ho.

*respective islands. In traditions concerning the song the contestants are
sometimes identified by name, and there is one (unlikely) tradition that
the Uist verses were made by Màiri nighean Alasdair Ruaidh.
Clanranald, who held South Uist, had their principal seat at Caisteal
Tioram in Moidart. The MacNeills, who ruled Barra, claim descent
from Niall Frasach and Niall Glùndubh, early kings in Ireland, and
their genuine chiefs include individuals named Gill Eòghanain and
Ruairi an Tartair: the latter died about 1620.*

[A' bhan-Uibhisteach:]

Fal iù o ho,
A Dhia! is gaolach
O hao ri ho ho,
Ri ho ho, ri ho ho,
Fal iù o ho.
A Dhia! 's gaolach
O hi a hao,   lium an gille,
     O hao ri ho ho,
     Ri ho ho, ro ho ho,
     Fal iù o ho.
     lium an gille,
     O hi a hao,
Dh'am bheil deirge is gile is duinnead:
Dalta nam bàrd thu 's nam filidh;
Ogha an fhir on Chaisteal Thioram,
Bheireadh air an togsaid sileadh,
Chan ann le bùrn gorm na linge,
Le fion dathte is e air mire,
Le fion thèidear cian ga shireadh.

[A' bhan-Bharrach:]

Ach eudail mhòr 's a Dhia fheartaich!
Càit an d'fhàg thu Ruairi an Tartair
No Niall Glùndubh no Niall Frasach,
Gill Eòghanain mòr an gaisgeach,
Chrathadh am flùr fo na martaibh,
Dhòirteadh am fion fo na h-eachaibh
Air ghaol bùrn nan lòn a sheachnadh,

[The Uist woman]

O God! Beloved to me is the young man

who has redness and whiteness and brownness:
you're the fosterson of poets and minstrels;
grandson of the man from Castle Tioram,
who would make the hogshead gush forth,
not with the blue water of the channel,
but with red wine streaming out sparkling,
wine that people travel afar seeking.

[The Barra woman]

But great treasure and miraculous Godhead!
Where have you left Ruairidh an Tartair
or Niall Glùndubh or Niall Frasach,
Gill Eòghanain, great the warrior,
who'd shake the flour under the cattle,
who'd pour the wine out for the horses
to spare them drinking puddle water,

Bheireadh cruithneachd dhaibh san fhrasaich,
Chuireadh srian an airgid ghlais riu,
Chuireadh cruidhean òir fo'n casan?

[A' bhan-Uibhisteach:]

A bhradag dhubh bheag a bhrist na glasan,
Fàgaidh mi ort an dubh-chapall!
Cha d'fhuaradh riamh staoileadh agaibh
Ach Barraidh dhubh bheag chrìon-dubh chlachach,
Oighreachd fhuair sibh bhuainn an asgaidh
Nuair a chunnaic Dia nur n-airc sibh,
Eilean fiadhaich am bi na fachaich,
E gun rùm 's gun fheur 's gun fhasgadh
'S e air fleòdradh leis na sgaitibh!

VI. Thugar Maighdeann a' Chùil Bhuidhe

This song seems to be only a fragment, but no other version is known to us. It was noted down by Alexander Carmichael from Mrs Flora Maclennan in Dornie, Kintail, sister of Captain Alexander Matheson (d. 1897) who compiled the Dornie manuscript collection (from which no. XXXI here is taken). Carmichael tells us that the subject is Christina MacCulloch, eldest daughter of MacCulloch of Park, near Dingwall (six poems by him are in the Fernaig manuscript). She was married to Fearchar MacRae (d. 1662), minister of Kintail, and was thus grandmother of Donnchadh nam Pìos, compiler of the Fernaig manuscript. Since the MacRaes were famous for their black beards (see line 8), Carmichael suggests that the poem dates from about 1611, when Christina married the minister and rejected the (anonymous) poet.

Thog am bodach air an each i,
Cha do lèidich e ro mhath i;
Buaram orm nan leiginn leis i
    Nan robh agam stòras.

Thugar maighdeann a' chùil bhuidhe,

who'd give them wheat in the manger,
put on them reins of grey silver,
put on their hooves golden horseshoes?

[The Uist woman]

Little black thief who broke the latches,
I will leave you with no comeback!
no title was ever found amongst you
but little, black, crinkled-black, stoney Barra,
land you got from us for nothing
when God saw you sore afflicted,
a desolate island full of puffins,
without a room or grass or shelter,
flooded, coming down with skate-fish!

VI. The maid of the yellow ringlets

Up on the horse the old man raised her,
not that his convoy was very fitting;
perdition take me if I'd let him keep her
if I had any riches.

The maid of the yellow ringlets,

Thugar maighdeann a' chùil bhuidhe,
Thugar maighdeann a' chùil bhuidhe
Dh'fhear bu duibhe feòsag.

Nan robh agam-sa an sin saidhbhreas,
Crodh is caoraich, greigh is goibhre,
Nàil, nar leiginn òigh an aoibhnis
Le fear foill no fòirneirt.

Thugadh taigh dhi ann an eilean
Far nach faiceadh i fear foille,
Far nach cluinneadh i guth coilich,
Far nach goir an smeòrach.

VII. Do Ruaidhri Mòr, Mac Leòid

Niall Mòr Mac Muireadhaigh

*Niall Mòr, of the MacMhuirich family of professional poets, probably
lived c.1550–c.1630, and this poem is in the strict form of*
rannaigheacht mhór. *He may have composed it following a visit to
Dunvegan in 1613 for the wedding of Iain Mùideartach (d.1670),
son of the Captain of Clanranald (Niall Mòr's patron), to Mòr,
daughter of Ruaidhri Mòr, chief of the MacLeods of Dunvegan.*

Sé hoidhche dhamhsa san Dún,
    níorbh é an coinnmhe fallsa fuar:
cuirm líonmhar ga hibhe a hór,
fionbhrugh mór is sine sluagh.

Teaghlach an tighe ar gach taobh,
    fá hí an fhine mheadhrach mhór;
feirrde suaimhneas ratha an ríogh
líon catha i n-uaignes fá ól.

Gáir na gcláirseach 's na gcuach dtrom
    ag nach gnáthach fuath ná feall,
gáir na mbleidhe fleasgach fionn,
lionn measgach is teine theann.

The maid of the yellow ringlets,
The maid of the yellow ringlets,
  is given to the blackest-bearded fellow.

Now, if I had then had riches,
cattle and sheep, goats and horses,
Forsooth, I'd never let the sweet maiden
  away with a trickster or tyrant.

A house has been given her on an island
where she could see no man to entice her,
where she would hear no cock crowing,
  where no thrush whistles.

VII. To Ruaidhri Mòr

Six nights for me in the fort,
it was no quartering false and cool:
liquor in plenty being drunk from gold,
great wine-hall of most venerable troops.

Members of the household all around,
that was the great and merry clan;
more certain is the bounty of the king
for the private drinking of a battle band.

Clatter of the harps and heavy bowls,
never accustomed to hate or deceit,
clatter of the wreathed, gleaming cups,
intoxicating ale and blazing fire.

Rí O nOlbhuir, aigneadh úr,
   connbhaidh a chaidreamh gach cliar;
'na ríoghbhrugh ní haisling ól
   dá shlógh líonmhar fairsing fial.

Fiche meisge linn gach laoi –
   nochar leisge linn ná lé;
fiú i neart ar mbeathaidh do bhí,
   ceathair, a trí, a seacht le sé.

VIII. Tàladh Dhòmhnaill Ghuirm

Probably a boat-song (iorram) *at first, this song survives as a waulking song, here in a South Uist version. The subject is usually assumed to be Dòmhnall Gorm Mòr (d.1617), chief of the MacDonalds of Sleat, but it might just as easily be his nephew and successor Dòmhnall Gorm Og (d.1643), the subject of no.XIX. The title implies that the song was composed when the subject was a child, but it is by no means certain that this was the case.*

Ar liom gura h-ì,
  Ho nàil ì bhò ho, a' ghrian tha ag èirigh
      Ho nàil ì ro ho ì.
'S i cur smala far nan reultan.
Tha mac mo rìgh a' dol na èideadh,
'S nuair thig mac mo rìgh tha an tìr-sa deiseil:
Chan ann le còig no le seiseir,
Ceud nan suidhe leat, ceud nan seasamh leat
'S ceud eile ri cur a' chupa deiseil;
'S nuair thèid mac mo rìgh an luing nan siubhal,
Chan e a' Mhòirthir as ceann uidhe dhut:
Ile is Cinn Tìre, an Fhraing 's a' Mhumhain.
Sin labhair a' bhean ris a' mhnaoi eile:
'Na, cò long ud steach on eirthir?'
'Don t'fhoighneachd ort! Cuma cheilinn?
Tha long Dhòmhnaill Oig, mo leanabh-sa ann:
Tha stiùir òir oirre is dà chrann eile dheth,

The King of Olbhur's fresh spirited line,
his patronage maintains every poet group;
in his palace drinking is no dream
for his great thronging generous troops.

Twenty times were we drunk each day –
neither we nor he from it did shrink;
a worthwhile fortifying of our lives,
four, three, seven and six.

VIII. Donald Gorm's Lullaby

I think it is the sun rising
casting a haze over the starlight.
My king's son is putting on his armour,
when my king's son comes, this land is ready:
not with five or with six men,
one hundred with you sitting, one hundred standing,
one hundred others passing the cup sunwise;
when my king's son boards the roaming vessel,
not Mòrar your destination:
Islay and Kintire, France and Munster.
Then the woman spoke to another:
'Now, what ship is that in from the coastline?'
'A curse on your asking! Why should I hide it?
It's Young Donald's ship, my nursling's:
she has two masts of gold, and a golden rudder,

Tha tobar fiona anns an deireadh aice
'S tobar fioruisge sa' cheann eile dhith.
Nàilibh, chuireadh mi mo theann-gheall
Ga b'e cala a bheil thu an Albainn
Gum bi mire ann, cluichd is gàire,
Bualadh bh ròg is leòis air dheàrnaibh
'S gum bi boineidean gorma air staing ann.'
Neart na cruinneadh leat, neart na grèineadh!
Neart na tuinneadh leat truime trèineadh!
Neart an tairbh dhuinn a bheir an sprèidh leat!
O, neart Oisein leat 's Osgair euchdaich!
'S gu robh a h-uile nì mar mi fhèin dhut:
Ach ma bhitheas cha bhuin beud dhut.

IX. Saighdean Ghlinn Lìobhainn

*Another song from the group of MacGregor songs which includes
no. III above. Once again, there is virtually no evidence available
to date it or identify its subject. There is an almost perverse lack of
evidence in the text itself: a MacGregor leader who has gone to the
Lowlands to fight is being praised, but we cannot even be sure
whether or not he has been killed (as the word* Bha *in the second
line might imply). It has been suggested that the word* ruaig *in the
second line might be written* Ruaig, *and might refer specifically to
'Ruaig Ghlinne Freòin', the Rout of Glenfruin (near Loch Lomond)
in 1603, when a MacGregor force defeated one commissioned by
the king and led by Alexander Colquhoun of Luss. This might lead
us to date the song to around that time, but there is no real evidence
for it.*

A mhic an fhir ruaidh
Bha gu misneachail cruaidh,
Do thuiteam san ruaig cha b'fheàirrde mi.

Triall gu dìreach
Re cois frìthe,
Bhiodh cuilìbheir dearbha leat.

a well of wine down at her stern-end
and a well of spring-water up at the other.
Forsooth, I would make a wager
whatever the harbour you call at in Scotland
there will be mirth there, sporting and laughter,
beatings with shoes and palms with blisters
and blue bonnets on a stand there.'
Might of the world with you, might of the sunshine!
Might of the waves with you of heaviest onrush!
Might of the brown bull that brings forth the cattle!
O, might of Oisean and valorous Oscar!
May everything be just as I am to you:
but if they are, no harm will touch you.

IX. The arrows of Glen Lyon

Son of the red-haired man
who was courageous and hard,
I were not better for your fall on the battlefield.

Travelling unswerving
along the edge of the moorland,
you would prove the worth of a culverin.

Coin air iallaibh,
Garg an gnìomhan:
B'e do mhiann bhith sealgaireachd.

Pìc nad dhòrnaibh
'S mill nas leòir oirr,
'S ann le treòir a thairngear i.

Glac nach leumadh
Re teas grèine
Agus cèir on Ghailbhinn oirr.

Ite an eòin lèith,
Brice na déidh,
Air a gleus le barbaireachd.

Sìoda à h-Eirinn
'S meòir ga rèiteach:
Cha tig brèin' fir cheàird air sin,

Ach fleisteir finealta
A Gleann Lìobhainn
Sìor-chur sìoda air chalpannan.

Cinn bhreac sgiathach
Air dhreach dialtaig:
Cha tig iarann garbhcail orr;

Gun chron dlùthaidh
Fod' làimh lùthmhoir,
Ite chùil is eàrr oirr sin.

An t-saoi nach sòradh
Bhith 'n tùs tòrachd:
'S mairg fear lòdail thàrladh ort.

An t-saoi nach aomadh
An tùs caonnaig,
Bhiodh sgian chaol on cheàrdaich ort.

Hounds on leashes,
ferocious in action:
hunting was your greatest happiness.

A bow in your fists,
studded with knobs,
its string drawn back with energy.

A quiver that would not burst
in the heat of the sun,
with wax from Galway made flexible.

Feather of the eagle,
a speckling behind it,
an arrow with barbed ornament.

Silk from Ireland
unravelled by fingers:
no rude tradesman will attain its excellence.

But a skilled fletcher
from Glen Lyon
winding silk round and round the swelling shafts.

Tails flanged and speckled,
the appearance of batwing:
iron, course and crude, comes nowhere near.

Unharmed by the straining
of your powerful handling,
on each arrow, a wing and tail-feather.

The warrior who would not refuse
a place in the vanguard:
woe to the clumsy man who would meet with you.

The hero who would not falter
at the onset of conflict,
a fine knife from the forge would accoutre you.

Triath na Sròine,
Mas fior dhomh-sa,
Gur i chòir as fheàirrde leat.

Dàimh gad mholadh,
Triall gu solar,
Bhiodh do sporan eàrlaidh dhoibh.

Beòir an cuachaibh,
Ol aig uaislean
Anns gach uair dh'an tàrladh sinn.

Pìob ga spreigeadh,
Fìon ga leigeil,
Luchd leadain re ceàrrachas.

Foireann air thì,
Dolaran sìos,
Galain dhen fhìon bhearcadach.

Cupaichean làn,
Musgair re dàimh,
Usgar air mnài airg-bhratach.

File à h-Eirinn
Seinn ort sgeula:
Thig còig ceud a shealltainn ort.

An t-òg as deise
Dh'fhalbh mu fheasgar:
Ghabh mi cead san anmoch dhiot.

An t-òg as sine,
As feàrr don chinneadh,
Nach d'rinn cillein airgid riamh.

Leam a b'aithreach
Gun bhith mar-riut,
Dol a sparradh Ghallbhodach.

Lord of Sronmilchon,
unless I am mistaken,
is the title which fittingly honours you.

Poet bands praise you,
journeying for provisions,
your purse was always prepared for them.

Beer in tassies,
being drunk by nobles
whatever the hour we visited.

Pipes inciting,
wine outpouring,
men with long tresses at backgammon.

On the board the pieces,
dollars wagered,
gallons of wine flowing seethingly.

Brimming goblets,
plenty for poets,
women in fine mantles with necklaces.

A high poet from Ireland
singing of your reputation:
five hundred will come to visit you.

The most accomplished young hero
who left in the evening:
in the late hours I took leave of you.

The most experienced hero,
best of the clansmen,
who never kept a secret silver hoard.

To me it was tragic
not to be with you,
setting off to rivet Lowland churls.

X. Cumha do Niall Og

Mòr NicPhàidein, a leannan

Niall Og was a son of Niall Mòr, brother of Eachann mac Iain Abraich, 5th Maclean of Coll (who is on record between 1536 and 1579). Niall Mòr was killed at An Clachan Dubh (line 12b) in Mull at the end of the sixteenth century, and Niall Og may have died, and been lamented in this song, between 1620 and 1625. But we have no evidence as to how he died, nor have we any further information about Mòr NicPhàidein.

Gur h-e mis tha air mo chùradh:
Thug mi gealladh don chùirteir
'S och, cha leig mi fo rùm e nios mò.

'S 'n àm tighinn don fheasgar
'S nach faic mi cuspair ga cheapail,
Mheudaich sùgradh nam fleasgach dhomh deòir.

Tha mi feitheamh na faiche
'S fir an òrdan dol seachad:
Fear t'aogaisg chan fhaic mi dh'an còir.

Duine uasal treun tapaidh,
Fear gasda ro bheachdail
Am fear fial dh'an do bhaist iad Niall Og.

Ach nam b'aithne dhomh t'àireamh,
B'ùr a' choill as na dh'fhàs thu –
Sìol nam failleanan àrd bu mhòr stoirm.

Mac Gill-eathain air thùs leat
Agus oighre na Cùladh;
'S leat Mac Fhionghain o dhlùthchoille chnò.

'S leat Mac Uimilein uaibhreach
'S Iarla Anntram seo chualas,
'S Lachainn thuit ann am bualadh nan sròn.

X. Lament for Niall Og

Mòr MacFadyen, his sweetheart

It is me who is tortured:
I've given a promise to the courtier,
and O! I will let him indoors no more.

At the coming of evening
when I see no target falling
the boys' mirth increases my tears.

I am lingering at the greensward
where the men march by in order:
in their company I see not one of your looks.

An aristocrat, strong and agile,
a fine man of good judgement,
the generous one they baptised Niall Og.

But if I know your measure,
fresh the woodland you sprung from –
seed of the mighty trunks of great storm.

MacLean with you in the vanguard
and the heir of Cùil, and also
Mackinnon from a dense wood of nuts.

With you proud MacQuillan
and, it is heard, the Earl of Antrim,
and Lachlann who fell when noses were struck.

Gura math thigeadh èileadh
Air an easgaid nach b'èidich
Nuair sgioblaicheadh m'eudail gu folbh.

Bu shealgair fèidh air an drùchd thu
'S trom a lotadh le t'fhùdar,
A' call na fala 's do chù air a lorg.

Bu tu 'n cearraich mòr prìseil
Air chairtean 's air dhìsnean:
'S tu gum buinneadh a' chìs air an torm.

Ach nam bitheadh tu maireann
Bu tu mo roghainn de dh'fhearaibh:
Leiginn Eòghann is Ailein air folbh.

A mhic Nèill bu mhòr gaisgeadh
A fuair a stialladh mun Chlachan,
'S e do bhàs chuir an fhadachd mhòr-sa oirnn.

Chunna mi do cheann cinnidh
'S càch gad ghiùlan gu Innis:
Gu robh sùrd ann air tiomadh gu leòir.

Bha gruaim mhòr air do dhalta
An àm an uaigh bhith ga treachailt –
Gu robh uair nach bu mhaslach siud dhò,

Thu bhith 'd chòmhnaidh sa' chaibeal
Gun chòmhradh gun chaidreabh
'S gun de chòmhnardachd leapa ach bòrd.

XI. Air Bàs mhic Mhic Coinnich

Donnchadh MacRaoiridh

This poem and the following three are taken from the Fernaig manuscript of 1688–1693 and are the only known surviving work of Donnchadh MacRaoiridh (d.c. 1630), who may have belonged to a

A kilt would look most handsome
on the thigh not misshapen
when my treasure made ready to depart.

The deer on the dew's huntsman,
heavy its wounding with your powder,
shedding blood with your hound on its track.

You were the respected big gambler
at cards and at dicing:
at the call of trumps the rent would be yours.

But if you were living
you'd be my choice of suitors:
I'd let Eòghann and Ailean away.

O son of Niall of great valour
who was scourged at the Clachan,
it is your death that cast us in deep gloom.

I saw the chief of your clansmen
as others bore you to Innis:
his mirth was quite unmanned.

Your fosterson was sorely troubled
when the grave was being deepened –
there was a time he would not have cared,

About you dwelling in the chapel
with no company or converse
with nothing flat for a bed but a board.

XI. On the Death of MacKenzie's Son

family of hereditary poets. Nos XI–XIII are all in a loose form of rannaigheacht mhór. *It seems likely that this poem is addressed to Cailean Ruadh (1597–1633), first Earl of Seaforth, on the death in 1629 of his only son, Alasdàir.*

Treun am Mac a thug ar leòn –
Cha bheir ar tòir air gu bràth;
Sinne gad a throgadh feachd,
Eisean is mò neart no càch.

Mhic Coinnich, deònaich do mhac
Don Fhear as mòr neart is brìgh:
Aig ro-mheud diadhachd do chuirp
Bheir Se dhuit a dhò no trì.

Do dheònaich Abram a mhac
San ìobairt fo smachd Mhic Dè;
Fuair e gràsan bho mo Rìgh,
An geall a-rìst aige fèin.

Air a' bhròn sin cuir-sa smachd –
Deònaidh Dia dhuit mac a-rìst
Dh'an robh sinn a' guidhe leat:
Cha chuibhe dhuit streap ri Crìosd.

Thug Dia dhuit urram is smachd
Air gach mac tha fodhad fèin;
Ris an anbhann cum-sa a' chòir:
Na leig leòn le duine treun.

Treun am mac etc.

XII. Rainn do rinneadh leis na shean aois

Donnchadh MacRaoiridh

The leaders lamented here have been identified as Cailean Cam (line 3a), chief of the MacKenzies, who died in 1594, and his sons (line 4a), Ruaidhri of Còigeach (1578–?1626) and Coinneach of Kintail

Mighty the Son who caused our wound –
   Him our pursuit can never reach,
even were we to raise a host:
   He is of greater power than all.

O Mac Coinnich, grant your son
   to the One of great virtue and strength:
for your body's godliness in return
   He will give you two or three.

Abram was willing to sacrifice his son
   in obedience to the Son of God;
favours he was granted from my King
   in return for this as a pledge to himself.

On that sorrow keep constraint –
   God will grant you a son again,
to Him we too have prayed
   it becomes you not to counter Christ.

God has given you the control and respect
   of every son in your command;
maintain the feeble in the Right:
   allow no wounding by a man of might.

XII. Verses made by him in his old age

(1569–1611). The final stanza is addressed to Coinneach's son and successor, Cailean Ruadh, who became first Earl of Seaforth in 1623 and died in 1633. Cailean Cam was buried at Manchainn (Beauly), and the later MacKenzie chiefs at A' Chananaich (Fortrose).

Fada ta mis an dèidh chàich
   'S an saoghal gu bràth dam reath,
Saoghal bha againn gus an-diugh
   Nach eil fios an-diugh cia fheadh.

An saoghal a bha againn uair,
   Gun ghoideadh e bhuainn gun fhios,
Agus an saoghal a tà,
   Gu dè phlàigh a nì sinn ris?

Dìth Chailein is tùrsach liom,
   Fear bho'm faighinn muirn gu bràth
Agus a bheireadh orm mios:
   Fada ta mis an dèidh chàich.

Dìth Ruaidhri is Choinnich fa thrì,
   A thuasgladh mì as gach càs,
Dh'fhàg mi fuireach ri mo sgrid:
   Fada ta mis an dèidh chàich.

Gun mhiann gun aighear gun cheòl
   Ach laighe fo bhròn gu bràth
Ach gu faigheam bàs gun fhios:
   Fada ta mis an dèidh chàich.

Ta fear am Manchainn nan lios
   Nach leigeadh mis as mu nì;
Do bhì an Cananaich nan clag
   Triùir a dh'fhàg gu lag mì.

Is mairg a ta beò nan dèidh
   'S a ta gun spèis fo bheil cion;
Thug an anshocair mo leòn
   Bho nach maireann beò na fir.

Long have I outlived them all
   with the world forever chasing me,
life that has been mine till today,
   it is not known how much longer now.

The life that once was ours,
   without warning it was stolen away,
and the life that still exists,
   what mess will I make of it?

For me Cailean's loss is sad,
   a man who always brought me cheer,
who on me bestowed great respect:
   long have I outlived them all.

The loss of Ruaidhri and Coinneach makes three
   who freed me from each awkward snare,
these have left me to await my last gasp:
   long have I outlived them all.

Devoid of desire or music or joy
   but lying forever morose
till death takes me unawares:
   long have I outlived them all.

There is a man in Beauly of the forts
   who never disappointed me with gifts;
in the Chanonry of the bells
   were three who have left me faint.

Woe to the one who them survives
   without respect underlaid by love;
the lack of solace has left me hurt
   since the men are not alive.

A Mhic Choinnich, Chailein òig
  Mhic an t-seòid nach robh gu lag,
A-nis bho is goirid mo theirm
  Bidh mis agad fèin gu fad.

                    Fad a ta mis etc.

XIII. Ceithir rainn do rinneadh leis an la a d'eug se

Donnchadh MacRaoiridh

Beir mise leat, a Mhic Dè,
  Agad fèin a b'ait leam tàmh;
Cum air do shlighe gu dlùth
  Mo chridhe is mo rùn 's mo ghràdh.

M'ùrnaigh agus m'aithrigh bhuan
  Bhith agad gach uair 's gach tràth;
Nar peacaidh uile leig linn –
  Tuilleadh cha dèan sinn gu bràth.

Achain eile dh'iarrmaid ort,
  Feudaidh do thoil-s' thobhairt dùinn:
An t-anam bhith agad fèin
  'S a' cholann chrè dhol san ùir.

Gu bhith air cathair nan àgh
  Cuide ri càch far a bheil,
Bho is tu as fiosraich mar a tàim
  Beir mise leat tràth is beir.

                    Beir mise leat etc.

O son of Coinneach, Cailean Og,
   son of the hero that was not weak,
since my term now is short,
   I will be entirely yours.

XIII. Four verses made by him the day he died.

Take me with You, O Son of God,
   with You would I gladly dwell;
keep these close to Your path:
   my heart, my desire and my love.

May my prayer and constant tears
   be with You now and always;
forgive me my every sin –
   none more can I ever commit.

Another boon of You I would ask,
   Your will can give it to me:
for You to keep the soul,
   when the body of clay goes in the earth.

To be at the throne of joy
   along with everyone else;
since You know best what I am like
   take me with you soon – do take.

XIV. Air Leabaidh a Bhàis

Donnchadh MacRaoiridh

Thàinig fàth bròin air ar cridhe
Nan dèanmaid deòr aithrighe;
 Gu bheil sinn salach uile
 De chion tola don Aon-duine.

An cridhe sin le'n salchar sinn
Ta na mheall talmhan sa' cholainn:
 Breugas e an fheòil uile leis
 Dhèanamh nas leòir d'ar n-aimhleas.

Sanntaichear leis na chì an t-sùil
Le gamhlas is le mìorùin
 Gu biathadh na colainn breugaich,
 'S gur e an talamh a h-ath-eudach.

Cha dleas mi breug a ràdh riut,
A chridhe-se ta cleith mo chuirp:
 Fàithne Dhè ga b'è do dhlighe
 Do mhiann fèin is iomchuidhe.

Mise an t-anam bochd tha am pèin:
Thèid mi nise thaigh Mhic Dè
 Is bidh mi dealachadh riut,
 Bho is talamh thu mar thàinig.

    Thàinig fàth bròin.

XV. Coisich, a Rùin

A version from Cape Breton island, Nova Scotia, of a waulking song which is also popular in the Hebrides: the singer was descended from Barra exiles. A date in the first half of the seventeenth century is possible, but there is no real evidence.

XIV. On His Deathbed

Misery was engendered in my heart
if I shed tears of penance;
   I am left utterly stained
   by lack of love for the Godhead.

That heart by which I am led to sin
is a lump of clay in the body:
   the whole flesh with this it will deceive
   into doing me plenty mischief.

It hungers for what is seen by the eye
with malice and with envy
   to feed the false flesh
   though earth be its next vestment.

It is not my duty to lie to you,
O heart that screens my body:
   though your duty were God's command
   your own will is more exacting.

I am a poor soul in pain:
I go now to the house of the Father,
   and from you I will depart
   since in earth you were engendered.

XV. Walk, my Dear

Cois-ich, a rùin ó ill, o ró, cum do gheall-adh; o hì e bhò, Bheir
sor-aidh bhuam, ó ill, o ró. dha na Hear-adh, bu hòir- eann o.

Coisich, a rùin,
ò ill orò,   cum do ghealladh;
          o hì e bhò
Bheir soraidh bhuam,
ò ill orò   dha na Hearadh,
          bu hòireann ò.
Gu Iain Caimbeul donn, mo leannan.
Sealgair geòidh thu, ròin is eala,
Bric a nì leum, 'n fhèidh nì langan.

'S fliuch an oidhche nochd 's gur fuar i.
Ma thug Clann Nill druim a' chuain orr,
Luchd nan seòl geal 's nan long luatha
'S nam brataichean dearg is uaine,
Chan fhear cearraig bheireadh bhuat i
No fear deaslaimh, mas i as cruaidhe.
Beannachd 'n sin dhan t-saor a dh'fhuaghail i:
Dh'fhàg e dìonach làidir luath i,
Aigeannach gu siubhal cuain i.

'S gur tric a laigh mi fo d'earradh:
Ma laigh, cha b'ann aig a' bhaile,
Duilleach nan craobh bhith gar falach,
Deatach a' cheò bhith gar dalladh,
Uiste fiorghlan fuarghlan fallain.

Gura mise tha air mo sgaradh!
Rèiteach a nochd bhith nad bhaile;
Ma tha, 's chan ann gus do bhanais
Ach gus do chur an ùir am falach
'N ciste chinn-chaoil, saoir ga barradh.

XVI. Iorram do Shir Lachann

Eachann Bacach

Very little is known about Eachann Bacach apart from the fact that he was a Maclean and is thought to have been maintained as a poet by Sir Lachlann Maclean of Duart (d. 1649). He may have been born

Walk, my dear,
            keep your promise;
take my greeting
            over to Harris,
to brown Iain Caimbeul, my sweetheart.
A hunter of goose, of seal and swan you,
of trout that leaps, of deer that bellows.

Wet the night tonight, and chilling.
If Clann Nill set off on the ocean,
the people of white sails and swift vessels
and of the red and the green banners,
no left-handed man could take her from you,
or right-handed man, if it were harder.
A blessing then to the wright who clinched her:
he left her strong, swift, willing,
a spirited one for sailing the ocean.

Often I lay beneath your mantle:
if I did, it was not at the homestead,
the leaves of the trees to keep us hidden,
the misty fog to keep us blinded,
pure-clean, cold-clean healthy water.

It is I who am rent asunder!
A betrothal tonight in your township;
if there is, it is not for your wedding
but to put you in the earth's keeping
in a narrow-ended cist, nailed down by the joiners.

XVI. *Iorram* to Sir Lachlann

around 1600 and his last datable song was composed in 1651. Here he praises Sir Lachlann, perhaps around 1635, and is possibly criticising his life-style to some extent in stanzas 3–4.

Mhic Mhoire na grèine,
A ghiùlain do cheusadh,
'S tu m'aighear is m'eudail 's mo threòir.

Greas thugainn dhachaigh
Oighre dligheach na h-aitribh,
Nam pìob is nam brataichean sròil.

An Dùn Eideann nan caisteal
Tha ceannard treun na mòr aitim:
'S ann de d' bheus a bhith sgapadh an òir;

Is nach b'urrainn do d' dhùthaich
Chur ad ghlacaibh de chùinne
Na chosgadh tu chrùintibh mun bhòrd.

Gur buidheach na h-èisgean
A dh'uasal an èididh:
Leat gun guidh iad buaidh threun anns gach tòir.

Chuid den chlèir-se chaidh seachad,
'S ann mu d' rèidhlean gum faighte iad;
'S fad 's is cian thug luchd astair ort sgeòil.

Crann gun doicheall gun euradh,
'S tric a chosgas na ceudan,
Dh'am bu dorsaireachd fèile tràth nòin.

Bhiodh fir Mhuile mu d' bhrataich,
'S ann mu d' ghualainn gum faighte iad;
Bu nì duilich am fasdadh 's do leòn.

Gun cruinnich mu d' bhrataich
Na curaidhnean gasda
Bheireadh fuil nuair a chaisteadh r'an sròin.

Son of Mary of the sunshine,
who suffered the Passion,
You are my strength, my treasure and my joy.

Speed to us homewards
the rightful heir of the dwelling,
of the pipes and the banners of silk.

In Edinburgh of the castles
is the chief of the great people:
one of your customs is the dispensing of gold;

Though never could your country
put in your hands the coinage
that you would gamble in crowns at the board.

Grateful the men of learning
to the noble of fine clothing:
your mighty triumph they implore in each pursuit.

Those of the poets who were passing
would be found about your greensward;
far and wide have travellers spread your fame.

Ungrudging bolt ready to open,
often spending hundreds,
at evening most welcoming your door.

The men of Mull would be at your standard,
they would be found at your shoulder;
to seize them and wound you would be hard.

They will gather round your standard
the valiant heroes
who would draw blood when noses would meet.

Bogha 'n iubhar dhearg-dhathte
Chùil bhuidh' thig à Sasann,
Ghabhadh lughadh 's nach spealtadh san dòrn.

Fiùbhaidh chinnteach chruaidh fhallain
'S i gun fhiar anns gach geal-laimh,
Bhith ga pianadh b'e leannan gach seòid.

Bhiodh na gallain bu daoire
Cruaidh sgalanta caoineil:
Glac eàrr is cinn ladhrach on òrd.

'S math do bharantan daonna
Gan aiseag far chaoiltean,
Clann bharrail dheas aobhaidh Mhic Leòid.

Mac Coinnich bu leat-sa e,
Bha e dìlis do d' phearsain:
Bha siod sgrìbhte ann an cart Chlann Ghill-Eòin.

XVII. Sona do Cheird, a Chalbhaigh

Cathal Mac Muireadhaigh

One of the last and greatest of the MacMhuirich family of professional poets, Cathal was composing before 1618 and after 1650, but not many details of his life are known. This poem has survived in a manuscript written by the poet himself, criticising a poet who, to judge by his name, An Calbhach, was probably an Irishman. Ronald Black has written of An Calbhach that 'he was clearly one of the new untrained or vernacular bards who were impinging on the professional poets' territory.'

Sona do cheird, a Chalbhaigh,
a ghiolla dhuinn dheaghadhbhraigh;
tarla d'onáir is d'ágh ort
gabháil re dán gan docracht.

A bow of red yew-wood,
with the yellow back from England,
that could be bent and not splinter in the fist.

A sure, hard, clean arrow
in each white hand held steady,
to strain it was the delight of each youth.

The most costly of saplings,
hard, resonant, well-seasoned;
a quiver of tails and heads grooved by the mall.

Fine your human warrants
being ferried across narrows,
the eminent, handsome, joyful Clan of MacLeod.

With you would stand MacKenzie,
he was loyal to your person:
that was written in a parchment of the MacLeans.

XVII. Blissful your trade, O Calbhach

Blissful your trade, O Calbhach,
brown youth of prospects substantial;
    you have met with honour and success
    in taking up poetry without effort.

Maith an ceird do thogh tusa
d'fhagháil muirne is macnusa,
   déanamh rann gan chóir gceartais
   a n-am óil is oireachtais.

As sona trá tarla dhuit,
gan amus d'fhoghlaim ordhuirc,
   bheith fa lán modha go mear
   le dán dona gan déanamh.

Dá n-íosta da mhéis do mhuic,
créad sin ach obair ordhuirc?
   Uaibhse dob fhearr ar domhan
   geall ar uaisle ag th'ealadhain.

Cur do bhriathar bun ós cionn
fuair sibh do choimeas choitchionn,
   's beith ar uair n-óla go leamh
   córa nó duan do dhéanamh.

Gé bhuailfeá fear an tighe
d'im nó d'fheoil go haingidhe,
   badh cóir scoláir do rádh ribh:
   clódh ar th'onáir ní héidir.

Níor chuir Dia ad dheoidh do dhochar
anmhuin ris an altachadh
   gan bhuain briuais da gach bord
   a n-uair niuais do neamhlorg.

Bheith a gcomaidh gach iarla
daoibhse as rabhadh rímhiadha,
   go cur ghreama muin ar muin
   's do theanga ag bleith re briathraibh.

Truagh trá nach dearna mise
amus ar iúl th'aistise,
   le céill gan cheart gan chuma
   's gan teacht ar fréimh foghluma.

Good the trade you have chosen
for winning cheer and luxury,
    making verses without right metrics
    at the time of drinking and revelry.

You are indeed in luck,
having made no stab at erudition,
    to be held in such respect, unabashed,
    with a mouldy, half-finished poem.

If you guzzled your pig off the plate
would that not be an amazing achievement?
    It would win you the greatest respect in the world
    for the nobility of your performance.

For getting your words mixed up
you have won quite a reputation,
    though clowning around on the booze
    is more your style than poetry.

Even if you were to hit your host
wantonly with meat or butter
    you would still be given a scholar's respect:
    it is impossible to detract from your honour.

God was not so hard on you
as to make you wait till grace is over
    before you swipe from each board the brose
    without as much as 'What's new?' to anyone.

Being in the company of each earl
for you is sign of high honour,
    piling in food, bite upon bite,
    while your tongue grinds out some phrases.

Alas I never made an attempt
on the lines of your metres,
    content devoid of truth or form
    and no reference to basic learning.

Tréigim dlaoi an dána dhírigh
mar fuair sinn sna seinlínibh,
   's bím at ord go nuaidhe a-nos:
   buaine iná an lorg dar leanas.

   Leanmhuin ghlún nginealach cáigh,
fios a n-einigh 's a n-iomráidh,
   dob fhearr dhúinn dul red tréidhibh
   's cúl do chur rér gcéidchéimibh.

Maith an tráth dá dhéanamh dhúinn
dá bhféadmaois, ar n-iúl d'iompúdh,
   's gan spéis ag duine dar ndán
   d'éis na cruinne do chaochládh.

Ceird an Chalbhaigh acht giodh cóir,
dul 'na seilbh budh dál dobróin;
   do-gheibh ór is annsa dhó-
   dhamhsa go mór as measo.

XVIII. A Sheónóid Méadaigh Meanma

Almost certainly by Cathal MacMhuirich, this poem survives in a manuscript he wrote at some time after 1649. It is addressed to Seònaid, wife of Dòmhnall Gorm Og, MacDonald of Sleat (and subject of no. XIX), on the death of their daughter Catrìona, which occurred between 1635 and 1640. Seònaid was a sister of Cailean Ruadh, first Earl of Seaforth (d.1633), and of Eoin (Iain), MacKenzie of Lochslin (d.1631).

A Sheónóid méadaigh meanma;
tuig thrá toil an Tighearna
   do dhéanaimh, a chnú chridhe,
   's tú d'fhéaghain dá oirbhire.

Let me forsake the snare of Strict Verse
as we found it in the tradition,
and let me enter your new order now:
it will last longer than the path I have followed.

Rather than tracing everyone's genealogy,
and knowing about their fame and generosity,
I would be better for taking up your arts
and turning my back on my early training.

This would be a good time for me to make,
if I could, a change in my profession
since no-one respects my gift
now that the world has altered.

However justified Calbhach's trade,
to engage in it would be a come-down;
his getting of gold – most dear to him –
makes matters for me much less blissful.

XVIII. O Seónóid, Be Of Good Cheer

O Seónóid, be of good cheer;
nut of my heart, understand now
that you must do His will,
and be wary of His displeasure.

Fuarais roimhe 'na ghrís ghoirte
bás Eóin is Iarla Síphoirte;
    is fios a reilge ar n-éag ann,
    ór fhéad nach feirrde bhur bhfulang.

Glac ó Dhia aoibhneas oile
i n-ionadh bhur n-eólchaire;
    beir buidhe do Dhia na ndúl;
    cia ar nach cluine caochlúdh?

Fa ní dá dhoilghe ar domhan
déana Iosa d'adhmoladh;
    gé bheith baoghal dhuid i ndán,
    tuig an saoghal ar seachrán.

Nar chualais riamh do ró gráidh
ó thús tochta an domhnáin –
    's é dá rádh riamh mar oideacht –
    nach biadh crádh 'na chomhuideacht?

Léig do Dhia bhur ndobrón díbh;
tiodhlaic t'inghean don Airdrígh;
    cuir sóláis céim tar chumhaidh,
    réim dóláis go ndiúltaighir.

Tréig th'imshníomh ar aigneadh mear,
ar mhuirn, ar mhacnas mhíleadh;
    a shubh fíneamhna, a ghéig ghlain,
    léig do mhímheanma ar mheadhair.

Tuig fós mar do dhearlaig dhúin
Rí na cruinne – is cúis iomthnúidh –
    a Mhac – ní h-é nárbh ionnráidh –
    is glac é mar eisiomláir.

Cuimhnigh mar do-chuaidh sa gcrann
Mac Dé dár ndíon a h-iofrann,
    meanma dár dtaobh mar do ghabh,
    go ndearna a thaobh do tholladh.

Before this, you received like burning coals
the deaths of Eóin and the Earl of Seaforth;
    knowledge of their graves after their decease
    could not have made your suffering easier.

From God accept other joy
in the place of your longing;
    give thanks to God of the elements;
    over whom do you not hear of changes coming?

However difficult the world
give praise to Jesus:
    though danger for you may be in store,
    understand the world is in error.

Heard you not this about excessive love –
recounted ever as a caution –
    that as long as the world has existed
    love has been accompanied by agony?

For God's sake desist from your grief;
to the High King grant your daughter;
    let mourning give way to joys,
    may you forsake your course of sorrow.

Abandon your care for high mirth,
for merriment, for dalliance with champions;
    O grape of the vine, O pure branch,
    your dejection supplant with gladness.

Understand too how the King of the world
gave us – a cause for envy –
    His Son – a fact worthy of note –
    take that as example.

Remember how He went on the Cross
to protect us from Hell, the Son of the Father,
    how He assumed care for us
    and let His side be punctured.

Is tuigthe fós dod ghnúis ghil
nach tug Dia dona daoinibh
   acht iasacht ar dhruim dhomhain,
   a dhiasfholt cruinn cladhamhail.

Cubhaidh dhuitse, a rosg ramhall,
dá n-éisde rém uraghall,
   laoidh d'fhagháil do chosg cumhadh
   's tosd i n-anáir ealadhan.

A dul ar neamh giodh leasg linn,
do Chaitir Fhíona is aoibhinn;
   maith an dícheal dá dreich ghlain
   bheith san rícheadh do roghain.

Maith an rogha rug sise
triall ón bheathaidh bhréigese
   go teagh na gclann gan choire
   thall i dteagh na trócaire.

A-tá i measg aingeal is ógh,
'na diaidh ní déanta dobrón,
   'na mionn shúl, ina gréin ghil
   gan phéin i ndún an Dúilimh.

Damadh tarbha dhí nó dhúinn
caoi chridhe fa cúis chaochlúidh
   do bhiadh leam cungnamh cumhadh
   le geall n-urrlamh n-ealadhan.

Gan mo thagra i n-ainmhibh mh'olc
guidhim Mac Dé le dúthracht
   fam shaoradh ó ghuin an gha
   ler taomadh fhuil ó Iosa.

                     A Sheón.

Let it be understood by you of fair face,
that God granted to mankind
  only a lease to the surface of the world,
  O furrowed hair like corn clustered.

It is proper for you, O languid eye,
if you listen to my discourse,
  to accept a lay to still grief
  and be quiet in respect for poetry.

Though her going to Heaven we deplore,
for Catriona it is glorious;
  good the zeal of her pure face
  allowing her by choice the Kingdom.

Good is the choice she made
to depart this life of falsehood
  for the house of the children without sin
  yonder in the House of mercy.

She is amongst angels and virgins,
we should not sorrow after her,
  she is a cynosure, a bright sun,
  without pain in the fort of the Creator.

If sadness of heart on account of her death
were to her or us of any profit
  I would have by me some help for grief
  in a ready promise of poems.

Not to charge me with the defects of my sins
I earnestly beseech the Son of the Father
  and to redeem me from the wound of the lance
  by which His blood was spilled from Jesus.

XIX. Oran do Dhòmhnall Gorm Og, Mac Dhòmhnaill

Iain Lom

Few solid facts are known about Iain Lom, perhaps the greatest and best-known of the vernacular poets of the seventeenth century. He was closely related to the ruling family of the MacDonalds of Keppoch – indeed his own family claimed seniority to them – and he seems to have regarded himself as an upholder of the traditional semi-political role of the poet. He may have been born around 1624 and perhaps died in the late 1690s, having commented in his songs on most of the century's political developments in the Highlands and in Scotland generally. This song was composed to Dòmhnall Gorm Og of Sleat, who died in 1643, and is possibly to some extent a student's exercise, a youthful learner's song of praise made according to the 'panegyric code'.

A Dhòmhnaill an Dùin
Mhic Ghilleasbaig nan tùr,
Chaidh t'eineach 's do chliù far chàch.

Tha seirc ann ad ghruaidh,
Caol mhala gun ghruaim,
Beul meachair bho'n suairce gràdh.

Bidh siod ort a' triall:
Claidheamh sgaiteach gorm siar;
Air th'uilinn bidh sgiath gun sgàth,

Is a' ghràbhailt mhath ùr
Air a toghadh on bhùth:
B'i do roghainn an tùs a' bhlàir.

A churaidh gun ghiamh,
Tràth ghabhadh tu fiamh
'S e thogadh tu sgian mar arm,

Is an gunna nach diùlt:
An tràth chaogadh tu an t-sùil
Gum bitheadh a shùgradh searbh.

XIX. Song to Dòmhnall Gorm Og, MacDonald of Sleat

O Dòmhnall of the Dùn,
son of Gilleaspaig of the forts,
you outstripped all in honour and renown.

There is benevolence in your face,
a slender brow without scowl,
a tender mouth of most affable love.

On campaign you carry these:
a sharp, blue, slanting sword;
on your elbow a gleaming shield,

And the helmet good and new,
selected from the stock:
it was your choice in the van of the charge.

O hero without fault,
when your anger was aroused
for weaponry you would take up a dirk,

And the gun that does not fail:
when you took aim with your eye
its merry-making was sure to be sour.

Is bogha an t-sàr chùil
Donn-mheallanaich ùir,
Caoin fallain den fhiùran dearg.

Is taifeid nan dual
Air a tarraing fo d' chluais:
'S mairg neach air am buailte a meall.

Is ite an eòin lèith
Air a sparradh le cèir:
Bhiodh briogadh an dèidh a h-eàrr.

Bho's imeachd don Fhèinn
Is cinn fhine sibh pèin
Air fineachan fhèil gu dearbh.

Iarla Aontraim nan sluagh
'S Clann Ghill-Eòin nam buadh,
Bidh siod leat is Ruaidhri garbh;

Mac Mhic Ailein nan ceud
'S Mac Mhic Alasdair fhèil
Is Mac Fhionghain gu treun nan ceann.

Creach ga stròiceadh,
Feachd na tòrachd
'S fir fo leòn nan arm.

Long ga seòladh,
Crith air sgòdaibh,
Stiùirbheirt sheòlta theann.

Beucaich mara
A' leum ri daraich,
Sùigh gan sgaradh teann.

Cha b'i an fhàsag
Ri sruth tràghaidh
'S muir na ghàir fo ceann.

And a bow with fine back,
brown-embossed and new,
of smooth, well-seasoned red wood.

And the bow's twined string,
drawn back below your ear,
woe to the one who would be hit with its force.

And a feather of the goose,
set in place with wax:
a prick after its tail passed through.

Since the Fian are gone
you are the leaders yourselves
of generous clans indeed.

The Earl of Antrim of the hosts
and the triumphant Clan MacLean,
and rough Ruaidhri – they will stand with you;

Clanranald, of hundreds, chief
and generous Glengarry's son
and fearless Mac Fhionghain as well.

Cattle being plundered,
a host pursuing
and men wounded by arms.

A ship sailing,
sheets quaking,
helm straining, set on course.

Roaring of the ocean
rushing at her timbers,
billows being cloven through.

She was no pea-pod
against the ebb-tide,
sea booming beneath her bows.

Thig loingeas le gaoith
Gu baile nan laoch
Gad a bhitheadh na caoiltean garbh,

Gu talla nam pìos
Far am faramaich' fion,
Far am falaichear mìle crann.

Bhiodh cruit is clàrsach
'S mnà uchd-àille
An tùr nan tàileasg geàrr;

Foirm nam pìoban
'S orgain Lìteach
'S cùirn gan lìonadh àrd;

Cèir na drillsean
Rè fad oidhche,
Ag èisdeachd strì nam bàrd;

Ruaig air dhìsnean,
Foirm air thìthibh
'S òr a sìos mar gheall,

Aig ogha Iarla Ile
Agus Chinn Tìre,
Rois is Innse Gall.

Clann Dòmhnaill nach crìon
Mun òr is mu nì,
Siod a' bhuidheann as prìosail geàrd;

Bho Theamhair gu I
Gus a' Chananaich shìos,
Luchd ealaidh bhon chrìoch nur dàil.

With a fair wind a fleet
comes to the home of the youths,
even though the narrows were rough.

To the hall of cups
where wine-quaffing makes din,
where a thousand bets are concealed.

A harp and a clarsach
and fair-bosomed women
in the tower of the short gaming boards.

The blasting of bagpipes
and Leith organs
with drinking horns filled to the brim;

Wax blazing
all through the nighttime,
as they listen to the contention of bards.

Dice being shaken,
pieces on tables
and gold thrown down as stake,

In the hall of the grandson
of the Earl of Islay,
of the Hebrides, Kintyre and Ross.

Clan Donald who never skimp
over cattle or gold,
the sept whose protection is most prized:

From Tara to Iona
to the Chanonry below,
you are visited by men of art.

XX. Oran air Latha Blàir Inbhir Lóchaidh eadar Clann Dòmhnaill agus na Caimbeulaich

Iain Lom

The battle of Inverlochy was fought on Sunday, 2 February 1645. The forces led by Alasdair mac Colla Chiotaich and James Graham, Marquis of Montrose, and including many MacDonalds, had finished their winter's slaughter in Argyll and marched northwards till they reached Cille Chuimein (Fort Augustus). There word was brought to them – by Iain Lom, it is said — that a Campbell force had entered Lochaber in pursuit and was burning the land. Montrose's army climbed eastwards over Cùil Eachaidh and into the hills, and then turned southwards, back towards Inverlochy (Fort William), and it appears from stanza 3 that Iain Lom was with the army at this point. They reached Inverlochy in the early morning and defeated the Covenanting/Campbell force in a bloody rout, which the poet evidently watched from rising ground above Inverlochy castle (stanza 2).

Hì rim ho ro, hò ro leatha,
Hì rim ho ro, hò ro leatha,
Hì rim ho ro, hò ro leatha,
Chaidh an latha le Clann Dòmhnaill.

'N cuala sibh-se an tionndadh duineil
Thug an camp bha an Cille Chuimein?
'S fada chuaidh ainm air an urram:
Thug iad as an naimhdean iomain.

Dhìrich mi moch madainn Dòmhnaich
Gu bràigh caisteal Inbhir Lòchaidh,
Chunnaic mi an t-arm dol an òrdugh
'S bha buaidh a' bhlàir le Clann Dòmhnaill.

Dìreadh a-mach glùn Chùil Eachaidh,
Dh'aithnich mi oirbh sùrd bhur tapaidh;
Ged bha mo dhùthaich na lasair
'S èirig air a' chùis mar thachair.

XX. A Song on the day of the Battle of Inverlochy

Hi rim ho ro, ho ro leatha,
Hi rim ho ro, ho ro leatha,
Hi rim ho ro, ho ro leatha,
The day was a victory for Clan Donald.

Have you heard about the bold return-march
made by the army that camped at Cille Chuimein?
Far has fame of their distinction been published:
they forced their enemies on before them.

I climbed early on Sunday morning
the brae of the Castle of Inverlochy,
I saw the army get into order
and victory on the field was with Clan Donald.

As you ascended the spur of Culachy
I recognised in you the frenzy of your courage;
though the land of my kindred was burning
what happened is compensation for the matter.

Ged bhitheadh iarlachd a' Bhràghad
An seachd bliadhna so mar tha e,
Gun chur gun chliathadh gun àiteach,
'S math an riadh o bheil sinn pàighte.

Air do làimh-se, a Thighearna Labhair,
Ge mòr do bhòsd as do chlaidheamh
'S iomadh òglach chinne t'athar
Tha an Inbhir Lòchaidh na laighe.

'S iomadh fear gòrsaid is pillein,
Chomh math 's a bha riamh de d' chinneach,
Nach d'fhaod a bhòtainn thoirt tioram
Ach foghlam snàmh air bun Nibheis.

Sgeul a b'aite nuair a thigeadh
Air Caimbeulaich nam beul sligneach,
H-uile dream dhiubh mar a thigeadh
Le bualadh lann an ceann gam bristeadh.

'N latha sin shaoil leo dhol leotha
'S ann bha laoich gan ruith air reodhadh;
'S iomadh slaodanach mòr odhar
Bha na shìneadh air Ach an Todhair.

Ge be dhìreadh Tom na h-Aire,
Bu lìonmhor spòg ùr bh'ann air dhroch shailleadh;
Neul marbh air an sùil gun anam
An dèidh an sgiùrsadh le lannan.

Thug sibh toiteal teth mu Lòchaidh,
Bhith gam bualadh mu na sròna;
Bu lìonmhor claidheamh claisghorm còmhnard
Bha bualadh an lamhan Chlann Dòmhnaill.

Sin 'n uair chruinnich mòr-dhragh na falachd
'N àm rùsgadh nan greidlein tana:
Bha iongnan nan Guibhneach ri talamh
An dèidh an lùithean a ghearradh.

Even if the earldom of Brae Lochaber
remained for seven years as it now is,
without sowing or harrowing or ploughing,
good is the interest by which we are compensated.

As for you, O Lord of Lawers,
though great your boasting of your broadsword
many a warrior of your father's people
is lying there at Inverlochy.

Many a fellow with cuirass and saddle
as fine as ever was in your kindred
was not allowed to get away dry-shod,
but learnt to swim in the mouth of the Nevis.

Yet more pleasing news kept coming
concerning the fate of the wry-mouthed Campbells:
as each of their bands made its appearance
their heads were battered in by sword-blows.

The day they had thought they would be triumphant
warriors were chasing them on frozen uplands;
there was many a great sallow sloucher
lying stretched out on Ach an Todhair.

Anyone who climbed the Look-out Hillock
could see many fresh paws badly salted;
over their lifeless eyes death's blankness,
after the slashing they got from sword-blades.

You made a hot attack round Lochy,
belabouring them hard on their noses;
many the sword, well-balanced, blue-fluted,
being wielded in the hands of Clan Donald.

Then there arose the great blood-letting
at the time of the drawing of slender rapiers:
the claws of the Campbells stuck into farmland
after the severing of their sinews.

'S lìonmhor corp nochdte gun aodach
Tha nan sìneadh air chnocain fhraoiche
On bhlàr an greaste na saoidhean
Gu ceann Leitir Blàr a' Chaorainn.

Dh'innsinn sgeul eile le fìrinn
Cho math 's a nì clèireach a sgrìobhadh:
Chaïdh na laoich ud gu'n dìcheall
'S chuir iad maoim air luchd am mìoruin.

Iain Mhùideartaich nan seòl soilleir
Sheòladh an cuan ri là doilleir,
Ort cha d'fhuaradh bristeadh coinne:
'S ait leam Barra-breac fo d' chomas.

Cha b'e sud an siubhal cearbach
A thug Alasdair do dh'Albainn,
Creachadh, losgadh agus marbhadh,
'S leagadh leis Coileach Srath Bhalgaidh.

An t-eun dona chaill a cheuta
An Sasann, an Albainn 's an Eirinn,
Ite à cùrr na sgèithe:
Gur misde leam ona ghèill e.

Alasdair nan geurlann sgaiteach,
Gheall thu an dè a bhith cur as doibh;
Chuir thu an raitreuta seach an caisteal –
Seòladh glè mhath air an leantainn.

Alasdair nan geurlann guineach,
Nam biodh agad àrmainn Mhuile
Thug thu air na dh'fhalbh dhiubh fuireach,
'S raitreut air pràbar an duilisg.

Alasdair mhic Colla ghasda,
Làmh dheas a sgoltadh nan caisteal,
Chuir thu an ruaig air Ghallaibh glasa
'S ma dh'òl iad càl gun d' chuir thu asda e.

Many the stripped corpse without clothing
lying sprawled over heathery hillocks
from the battle where the heroes were incited
right to the end of Leitir Blar a' Chaorainn.

I could faithfully tell another story
as well as any cleric will write it:
those warriors did their utmost
and left their enemies utterly stricken.

Iain of the sparkling sails of Moidart
who on a gloomy day would sail the ocean,
you were never found to break a promise:
I am delighted you hold Barbreck in your power.

That was no faulted manoeuvre
Alasdair mac Colla made to Scotland,
burning, killing, wreaking destruction,
broken by him the Cock of Strathbogie.

The wretched bird that lost its appearance
in England, in Scotland and in Ireland,
he is a feather from the wing-pit:
I am disgusted since he has submitted.

Alasdair of the sharp lopping sword-blades,
yesterday you promised you would destroy them;
you sent their retreat past the castle –
that was an excellent way to chase them.

Alasdair of the pointed sword-blades,
if you had with you the Mull heroes,
you could have stopped those ones escaping
of the dulse-fed rabble when retreating.

Alasdair, son of generous Colla,
a skilled hand at splitting castles,
you routed the Lowland cowards
and the kale they drank, you made them skitter.

'M b'aithne dhuibh-se an Goirtein Odhar?
'S math a bha e air a thodhar:
Chan inneir chaorach no ghobhar
Ach fuil Ghuibhneach an dèidh reodhaidh.

Sgrios oirbh mas truagh leam ur càradh,
'G èisdeachd anshocair ur pàisdean,
Caoidh a' phannail bha anns an àraich,
Donnalaich bhan Earra-Ghàidheal.

XXI. Turas mo chreiche thug mi Chola

This song is one of the very few which offer something of a Campbell view of the events of 1644–45. It looks like a waulking song in structure, and there are several widely divergent versions. One editor has stated, probably with excessive certainty, that the song was composed by Fionnghal, wife of Iain Garbh, 8th Maclean of Coll. She was a sister of Campbell of Achnambreac, Sir Donnchadh, who was killed leading the Covenanting army at Inverlochy; and her son, Eachann Ruadh, later 9th of Coll, fought on the Royalist side there. Possibly the Seònaid in line 9 is Fionnghal's own daughter.

> *Hì ri o ho, luidh leo iù bho,*
> *Hì ri o hì rì o luidh leo,*
> *Hì ri o ho, luidh leo iù bho,*
> *Hì ri o luidh leo, iù bho luidh leo.*

Turas mo chreiche thug mi Chola
Shealltainn air caisteal gun solas:
Rinn iad mo leaba aig an doras
Fo chasan ghillean is chonaibh.
Rinn iad siod is rud bu dona –
Thug iad mo bhràiste as mo bhrollach
'S usgraichean mo chneapan solais,
Fàinneachan daoimein mo chorrag:
Thug iad siod do Sheònaid dhona.
Chan fhaicear a mac fo bhoineid
No òigridh a' dol na coinneamh.

Did you know the Goirtein Odhar?
it has received a fine manuring:
neither with sheep-dung nor goat-dung
but with Campbell blood after congealing.

Destruction take you if I pity your condition,
as I listen to the misery of your children,
lamenting the mob who were in the battle,
the howling of the women of Argyll.

XXI. The Journey of my undoing I made to Coll

The journey of my undoing I made to Coll
to visit a castle without lamplight:
they made up my bed at the doorway
under the feet of curs and servants.
They did that and a deed that was yet worse –
they took my brooch out of my bosom
and the gems of my shining necklace,
the diamond rings of my fingers:
those they gave to wicked Seonaid.
Her son is not seen in a bonnet
nor young men going to meet her.

Chaidh iad don t-searmoin Di-Dòmhnaich
'S dh'fhàg iad san taigh bhàn mi am ònar
'S an tubhailte chaol ma m' dhòrnaibh
'S mi an ceangal am fuil gu m' bhrògan,
'S gum b'e fuil mo bhràithrean òga.

B'ann agam fhèin a bha na bràithrean
Bu doinne ceann 's bu ghile bràighe,
Is an dà ghruaidh mar ròs an gàrradh
'S am beul cho dearg ris an sgàrlaid.

'S gura mise tha air mo sgaoile
Ma Mhac Dhonnchaidh Ghlinne Faochain:
Chuir iad e do Chille Bhaodain
An craiceann nan gobhar gaoiseid.
Cha b'ionann 's a bhith 'n Inbhir Adhradh:
Gheibhte mnathan òga gad chaoine,
Slios am boineid air an aodann,
Gruagaichean 's an cuailean sgaoilte
Eadar Sòraba is an Caolas,
Eadar siod is Tobhta Raghnaill.

Cheangail iad mi air sgeir mhara,
Feitheamh iasgairean a' chladaich.

'S gur e mise tha fo mhulad:
Chì mi na h-eòin air an rubha,
Cluinnidh mi an sgreuch 's an guileag
Gun duine staigh bheireadh fuil orr.
Mo cheist air gìomanach a' ghunna
Bheireadh air an earba fuireach,
An ròn maol re taobh na tuinne
Is an eala bhàn as binne luinneag.

Ach nam faighinn siod a chur an òrdugh,
Eachann Ruadh a chur air ròsta
Air dìol na muice duibhe dòite
No dìol na circe thig on chòcair!

On Sunday they went to the sermon
and left me alone in the deserted building,
my wrists bound with the fine-woven towel,
down to my shoes in blood, fettered,
and that was the blood of my young brothers.

They were my own, those brothers,
heads the brownest and throats the fairest,
their cheeks like a rose in a garden,
mouths red as cloth of scarlet.

It is me who is shaken
about Mac Dhonnchaidh of Gleann Faochain:
they buried him in Cille Bhaodain
in a hairy hide of goatskin.
In Inbhir Adhradh that would not have happened:
young women would be found to keen you,
their bonnets pulled down over their faces,
girls with their hair loosened
between Soraba and Caolas,
between there and Tobhta Raghnaill.

They put me in bonds on a sea skerry,
waiting for the fishermen of the seashore.

It is me who is in sorrow:
I see the birds on the headland,
I hear their screeching and mewing
and have no man to leave them bloodied.
My love the hunter with the musket
who would make the roe-buck falter,
the smooth-headed seal beside the wavetops
and the white swan of the sweetest whooping.

If I could only make this happen:
Eachann Ruadh to be set roasting
given the scorched black pig's treatment
or the handling the cook gives the chicken!

Eachann Ruadh a dhol an dolaidh
'S nìor faiceam a chlann mun doras
No a chuid mhac a' dol na choinne!

Gur e mise ta air mo shiorradh
Mun oighre ud Cheann Locha Giorra,
Achnambreac is Bràighe Ghlinne,
'S Càrn Asairidh anns am bi na gillean,
Marcaich nan each steud 's nam pillean.

XXII. An Cobhernandori

The title here has been interpreted as representing Cobhair nan Tory,
*'the help to the Tories', but this is open to question on various grounds.
For one thing, if the word* Tory *really were present it would apparently
be the earliest attested use of the word in English as a term of political
abuse. Whatever the etymology of 'Cobhernandori', the text of the song
allows the suggestion that the word denotes a political group usually
known as the 'Engagers'. These were Covenanters among the Scottish
establishment, who in 1648 'engaged' to support the king (now in
prison in the Isle of Wight) on condition that he gave Presbyterianism
a three-year trial in England. At Preston in England in August, an
Engager army of 14,000 or more was forced to surrender to (the poet
says) 7000 troops under Cromwell. The 'Kirk Party', opponents of the
Engagers, then proceeded to purge the Church of ministers who had
supported the Engagement. One of the Engagers' military leaders was
Lieutenant-General John Middleton, who had fought against Mon-
trose at Philiphaugh in 1645. Aonghas, 9th MacDonald of Glengarry
(d.1680), who had fought in Ireland with the 'Confederate Catholics'
and been imprisoned there, returned to Scotland late in 1648 or early
in 1649, but shortly afterwards – about the time of the composition of
this song – went into further exile in Holland. The final lines here
almost certainly refer to Alasdair mac Colla (d.1647), for the text in
the manuscript ends with four lines of a further stanza (omitted here)
about Alasdair.*

Eachann Ruadh to be ruined
and let me not see his children round the threshold
or his sons going to meet him.

It is me who is distracted
on account of that heir of Ceann Locha Giorra,
of Achnambreac and Braigh Ghlinne,
and Carn Asairidh where the youths are,
rider of chargers and war-horses.

XXII. The Engagers

An oidhche nochd gur fada leam
  'S mo bhreacan air mo ghruaim,
Mu d' dhèibhinn, Aonghais Gharanaich,
  A dhealaich ruinn Di-luain;
'S eagal leam gun tàlaidhear sinn
  Don Olaind thall thar chuan,
Ach masa tuille fògraidh dhuit
  Thig air mo ròibein ruadh.

Sgrios air a' Chobhernandori
  Nach do thionntaidh iad san tìm;
Ge mòr ar ruith re prionnsachaibh
  Gum b'annsa linn an t-sìth;
Chuaidh sibh 'n leth an Ainspioraid
  Le ur bainn gan cur am prìs,
'S chan fhoghnadh sud don phrionnsadh
  Ged a chionnsaich iad an rìgh.

Claidheamh geur cha ghiùlain mi,
  Ga rùsgadh as a thruaill;
Gun tugainn do dh'fhear saothrach e
  Chur faobhair air a thuaigh;
Gum b'annsa bhith le caibeachaibh
  A' ruamhradh geig sa' chluain
Na strì re cogadh leth-cheannach
  'S a' teich' air feadh nam bruach.

Tha masladh mòr is mì-chliù
  Air tighinn on Chrìch nar n-uchd:
Ar n-armailt air a strìocadh
  Le seachd mìle marcach trup,
Ar ministearan sgìreach
  Mar bhràighdean mìn-gheal mult
Is oighre nan trì rìoghachdan
  Am prìosan an Eilean Uicht.

This night tonight is long with me,
  with my plaid up over my scowl,
because of you, Aonghas Garanach,
  who on Monday from us did part;
Across the sea to the Netherlands
  I fear we will be drawn,
but if longer exile is in store for you
  it will reflect on my red beard.

    Destruction on the Cobhernandori
      that they did not turn in time;
    though great our exertion for potentates,
      we would much prefer peace;
    you fought on the side of the Evil One
      with your bonds going up in worth,
    but the prince would not be satisfied
      even if they controlled the king.

A sharp sword I will not take up,
  brandishing it from its sheath:
I would give it to a husbandman
  to put an edge on his axe;
Far better working with turf-cutters
  digging a trench in the field
than fighting in a shambolic war,
  and fleeing across the hills.

On us great shame and disrepute
  from the Border have come:
our army having surrendered
  to seven thousand mounted troops,
in the parishes our ministers
  like captive soft white sheep,
and the heir of the three principalities
  in prison in the Isle of Wight.

A Middleton nan cùirtean
Bu mhòr mo dhiùm an tosach ort-sa:
Bha thusa anns a' chùirt ud
Is gun dùraiginn do chrochadh;
Cha b'ionann thu is an spailp fiùghantach
Nach faighteadh lùb na fhocal
'S nach bitheadh fui smachd ùmaide
Aig ùdlaich nan cranna forca.

XXIII. Bithidh 'n Deoch-sa an Làimh mo Rùin

Mac Mhic Ailein, the Captain of Clanranald, discovered that his daughter was determined to marry a servant, and he ordered that she be left on a rock to drown. Maclean of Coll, passing by, rescued her from the rock and took her as a servant to Coll. A long time afterwards, the new Mac Mhic Ailein, her brother, was invited as a guest to Coll, and the girl was serving at table. She was asked to sing at the meal and she sang this song. Mac Mhic Ailein fell in love with her, but she explained that she was his sister and he took her home with him to Uist.

(That is one of a variety of traditional tales told to explain this song and some items of its different texts.)

Sguiridh mi nise den t-seisreach:
Thàine feasgar a leagadh driùchd.

Bithidh 'n deoch-sa an làimh mo rùin,
Deoch slàinte le fear an tùir,
Bithidh 'n deoch-sa an làimh mo rùin.

Sguiridh mi threabhadh na fiadhair
Bho nach d'fhiadhaich iad mi 'n dùn.

Dh'òlainn deoch slàinte mo thighearna:
'S tu thighinn niar bu mhath liom.

O Middleton of the palaces
   my displeasure was first with you:
when you were attending yonder court
   I would love to have seen you hanged;
you were no match for that worthy beau
   in whose words was found no twist
and who would not be humiliated
   by the forky-antlered stag.

XXIII. This Drink will be in the Hand of my Dear

Sguir-idh mi nis-e den t-seis-reach: Thàine feasg-ar a leag-adh driùchd.

Bith-idh 'n deoch-sa an laìmh mo rùin, Deoch slàin-te le fear an tùir Bith-idh 'n deoch-sa an làimh mo rùin.

I will now give up the ploughing:
evening has come to drop the dew.

    This drink will be in the hand of my dear,
    good health to the lord of the tower,
    this drink will be in the hand of my dear.

I will stop ploughing the lealand
since they did not invite me to a fort.

I would drink to my lord's well-being:
your coming east would make me glad.

Oladh no na òladh càch e,
Bidh mo chàrt-sa aig ceann a' bhùird.

'S dàna leam a ghabh thu am balach
Air Mac Mhic Ailein nan crùn.

B'e sud am mac a b'fheàrr na d'athair
'N iomairt 's am maise is an cliù.

'S cha b'e na pocannan mine
Gheibhte orra ghillean gu bùth;

Sgian bhreac nan dual air an slinnean,
Snaidhm gu h-imrich air a cùl.

'S ged tha mise an so an Cola,
B'e mo thoil a dhol a Rum,

Asa sin a-null a dh'Uibhist
Far am buidhicheadh an lionn.

M'fheudail thu, muime nam macan,
Làmh gam altram air a glùn.

'S toigh leat pèidse de Chlann Mhuirich:
'S ann leat urram na thèid a-null.

XXIV. Oran do Thighearna Ghrannt

Seumas MacGriogair

Seumas Grant (1616–1663) succeeded as 7th of Freuchie, near Grantown-on-Spey, and chief of the Grants, in 1637, and he was married in 1640 to Mary Stewart (d.1662), whose mother, Anne Gordon, was daughter of George, first Marquis of Huntly (d.1636), and of Henrietta, daughter of Esme Stewart, second Duke of Lennox (c.1542–1583). We have no evidence on which to date the song closely, but it is at least possible that it dates from shortly after the marriage. Nothing seems to be known for certain about the poet.

Whether or not the others will toast him,
my quart will be at the top of the board.

I think it outrageous you chose the youngster
before Mac Mhic Ailein of the crowns.

That was the lad who bettered your father
in bearing and in beauty and renown.

And it was not sacks of corn-meal
your boys were found carrying to the shop.

A wrought chequered knife on their shoulders,
a knot to slip it at the back.

Though I am in Coll here waiting,
I long to go to Rum,

From there over to Uist
where beer would be dispensed.

You are my treasure, nurse of the heroes,
a hand dandling me on her knee.

You are fond of a page of Clann Mhuirich:
all who go across hold you in esteem.

XXIV. A Song to Lord Grant

Lìon mulad mi fèin
Bho m'fhuireach an dè,
Me chumail ri clèith,
Beart bu duilich leam fèin
'S nach b'fhasan leam è 's gach uair.

Slàn iomradh do m' ghràdh
So chunna me an-dràsd,
Ceann buidhne gun sgàth –
Cha Dhuibhneach a tà me luaidh.

Ach soiridh uam fèin
Nunn do Shrath Spè
Gu talla an fhir fhèil,
Ceann uidhe nan ceud:
'Se Seumas do'n gèill na sluaigh.

Dhom-sa b'aithne do bheus,
A lasgaire thrèin:
'N àm laighe don ghrèin
(Mar bharail dom fèin),
Bhiodh solas le cèir,
Bhiodh faram nan teud nad chluais.

Dhom-sa b'aithne
Beus do bhaile:
Cùrsain ghearra,
Cùird d'an caradh,
Steudaibh meara,
Srèin d'an tarrainn
Ri greighean bu ghlaine snuadh.

Dìreadh bruthaich,
Pìc dhen iubhar
Sìnte riutha,
Glaca dubha
Dhèanadh pudhar:
Luaidhinn gum b'e t'fhuaim.

I am filled with hurt
as yesterday I was stuck,
kept at the plough,
for me hard work
since at no time was that my wont.

Good health to my love
I saw here just now,
fearless leader of troops –
no Campbell do I intend to praise.

But a greeting from myself
across to Strath Spey
to the princely man's hall,
for hundreds their goal,
it is to Seumas the hosts succumb.

I knew your ways,
O brave young man:
when the sun went to rest
as I did too,
there'd be candle-light,
the sound of strings in your ears.

I was well acquainted
with the ways of your household:
short racespans,
reins thrashing,
spirited stallions,
bridles straining
towards mares of the fairest form.

Climbing the hillside,
a bow of yew-wood,
stretched out alongside,
with black quivers
that would cause mishap:
I would say that that was your style.

'N Eilginn nan Gall
Bhuinnigeadh tu an geall;
Dh'fhuilgeadh tu spàirn
'S nach cunntadh tu an call
Mun leigeadh tu an cabhsair uait.

Dh'fhaighte an t'àras
Ceòl nan clàrsach,
Fòirne air thàilisg,
Mnà uchd-àillte
As crùin an geall mun cuairt,

Bhiodh cùirn cheàrnach
Air cruinn deàrna,
Gu dlùth deallran,
'N teidheadh mòr-àighear
An cliù Alba:
Cha siod àirde am fuaim.

Aig ogha an t-seanair
An robh 'n t-eineach,
Ma'n rith pannal;
Garbh re leanail
Cliù is aithne
Iomadh ceannas sluaigh.

Mary Stuart,
Iar-ogha an Diùc thu,
Ogha Mhorair Hùnndaidh,
O shìol chrùin –
Gu meal thu t' rùn on fhuair.

Gruaidh mar ubhal
As dearg rudhadh
Air fiamh an iubhair
'N àm a lughadh,
Fo shaighead cur siubhail:
Cùl as buidhe dual.

In Elgin of the Gaill
you would win the bet;
the contest you would stand
and not count the loss
before leaving the streets behind.

In your house could be counted
music of the clarsach,
a crowd at the gammon,
fair-bosomed women
and crowns being wagered all round.

Square-cut goblets
in palms rounded,
gleaming densely,
pleasure being taken
in Scotland's reputation:
that was not the height of their din.

Grandson of the grandfather
who enjoyed much honour,
women cluster around him;
hard to follow
his fame and recognition,
his leadership of many a host.

Mary Stewart,
you're the Duke's great grandchild,
grandchild of the Marquis of Huntly,
from the Crown descended,
since you have him, may you enjoy your love.

Cheek like an apple
flushed russet,
the colour of yew-wood
at the time of flexing
to send forth an arrow,
hair of the yellowest of curls.

XXV. Chailin òig as Stiùramaiche

A popular waulking song whose second refrain line originates in a lost sixteenth-century Irish song, and the theme may consist of relics of a ballad. None of the extant versions ever amounts to a complete coherent text, but Dr Campbell of Canna has identified five parts common to many versions, including ours: (a) a young man meets a girl who makes excessive requests of him; (b) he is ill with a fever for 15 months, after which the girl comes to ask how he is, and he tells her; (c) presumably as a result of her visit, he recovers, and scores well at shinty; (d) he complains of the fickleness of women, comparing them to various unstable creatures and phenomena; (e) the young man says that a dairymaid is the better of having a herdsman, who can do certain things for her (implying a reconciliation). In this version, part (e) comes first.

Cailin mise, buachaill thusa,
   Chailin òig, a hù ra bhò hò,
Cailin mise, buachaill thusa,
   Chailin òig as stiùramaiche,
B'fheàrrde banchaig buachaill aice,
   Chailin òig, a hù ra bhò hò,
Ged nach dèan e ach falbh reimpe;
Thèid e mach san oidhche fhrasaich,
Chuireadh e na laoigh am fasgadh,
Ghabhadh e gu suanach aca.

Latha dhomh 's mi falbh an fhàsaich,
Thachair orm-sa an donn-bhean dhàna;
Shuidh sinn air cnoc, rinn sinn bànran;
Dh'iarr a' chailin nì nach b'fheudar –
Muileann air gach sruth an Eirinn,
Caisteal air gach cnocan grèineadh.

XXV. 'Calen O Custure Me'

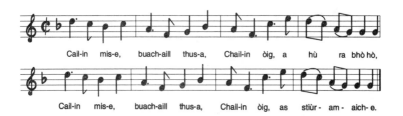

Cail-in   mis-e,   buach-aill   thus-a,   Chail-in   òig,   a   hù   ra   bhò hò,

Cail-in   mis-e,   buach-aill   thus-a,   Chail-in   òig,   as   stiùr - am - aich- e.

I am a girl, you are a cowherd,

I am a girl, you are a cowherd,

a milkmaid is the better for a cowherd,

if all he does is go before her;
he will go out on a showery night,
he would put the calves in shelter,
he would go about them quietly.

One day as I crossed the moorland,
I was met by a bold brown woman;
we sat on a hill, we made lovetalk;
the girl asked for something not possible –
a mill on every stream in Ireland,
a castle on each sunny hillock.

Chaidh mi dhachaigh 's laigh mi an là sin
'S thug mi bliadhna mhòr is ràithe
Ann an teasach na plàghach.

Dh'èirich mi an ceann nan còig ràithean;
Thàinig ise, an donn-bhean dhàna,
Dhìrich i an staidhir a b'àirde,
Ghlac i ursann as gach làmh dhi,
Dh'fhoighneachd i gu dè mar bhà mi.

'Tha mi gu bochd truagh mar 's àbhaist,
Olc le m' charaid, 's math le m' nàmhaid!'
'Ghràdh thu, b'fheàrr liom agam slàn thu!'

Chaidh mi mach air feadh na sràideadh,
Ghlac mi an caman, chuir mi pàm leis;
Ma chuir mi h-aon, chuir mi dhà leis.

Ach mur h-e gur bean mo mhàthair
'S gur h-e mo mhuime rinn m'àrach,
Dh'innsinn sgeul bheag air na mnài dhuibh:
Tha iad sgeigeil, bleideil, bàrdail
'S an aigne mar ghaoth a' Mhàrta,
Mar uan Chèitein anns a' mhèilich,
Mar laogh fèidh an dèidh a mhàthar,
Mar mhuir a' lìonadh 's a' tràghadh,
Mar easgann an lodan làthchadh.

XXVI. Oran Cumhaidh air Cor na Rìoghachd

Iain Lom

The poet grieves for the death of Alasdair mac Colla in 1647 (stanza 2) and bemoans the fact that king Charles II, crowned on 1 January 1651 at the age of 20, is powerless. James Graham, Marquis of Montrose, had been betrayed by Niall MacLeod of Assynt (whose father was also named Niall) and beheaded in Edinburgh on 21 May 1650. After the battles of Inverkeithing and Worcester in 1651 (in which the Macleans, Buchanans and MacLeods suffered severe losses) Scotland came firmly under the control of Oliver Cromwell's English parliament.

I went home and that day lay supine
and spent a whole year and a season
beset by the plague, in a fever.
I rose up after five seasons;
she came, the bold brown woman,
she climbed the stairs to the topmost,
in each of her hands she gripped a door-post,
she asked me how I was fairing.

'I am as usual poor and wretched
to my friend's sorrow, my enemy's relish!'
'You love, I'd prefer you got better!'

I went out and wandered the highway,
I grabbed the shinty stick, I shot a goal with it;
If I shot one, I shot a couple.

But if it wasn't that my mother is a woman
and it was my nurse who raised me,
I could tell you a thing or two about women:
they are mocking, fawning, pompous,
their disposition like the Marchwind,
like a little May lamb bleating,
like a deer-calf seeking its mother,
like the sea filling and ebbing,
like an eel in a muddy puddle.

XXVI. A Lament for the State of the Country

Mi gabhail Sraith Dhruim Uachdair,
'S beag m'aighear anns an uair so:
Tha an latha air dol gu gruamachd
    'S chan e tha buain mo sproc.

Ge duilich leam 's ge dìobhail
M'fhear cinnidh math bhith dhìth orm,
Chan usa leam an sgrìob-s'
    Thàinig air an rìoghachd bhochd.

Tha Alba dol fo chìoschain
Aig farbhalaich gun fhìrinn
Bhàrr a' chalpa dhìrich –
    'S e cuid de m' dhìobhail ghoirt.

Tha Sasannaich gar fairgneadh,
Gar creach, gar murt 's gar marbhadh;
Gun ghabh ar n-Athair fearg ruinn –
    Gur dearmad dhuinn 's gur bochd.

Mar a bha Cloinn Israel
Fo bhruid aig rìgh na h-Eiphit,
Tha sinn air a' chor cheudna:
    Cha èigh iad ruinn ach 'Seoc'.

Ar rìgh an dèidh's a chrùnadh
Mun gann a leum e ùrfhas,
Na thaisdealach bochd rùisgte
    Gun gheàrd gun chùirt gun choist;

Ga fharfhuadach as àite
Gun duine leis de chàirdean,
Mar luing air uachdar sàile,
    Gun stiùir gun ràimh gun phort.

Cha tèid mi do Dhùn Eideann
O dhòirteadh fuil a' Ghreumaich,
An leòghann fearail treubhach
    Ga cheusadh air a' chroich.

As I travel the Strath of Drumochter,
little my joy at this season:
the day has turned out grimly
   and that does not help my gloom.

Though I feel it a hard deprivation
to be lacking my good kinsman,
no easier borne is this mishap
   that has overcome the poor land.

Scotland is under tribute
to foreigners without justice
above the right taxation –
   that is part of my sore plight.

We are plundered by the English,
despoiled, slain and murdered;
we must have caused our Father anger –
   for we are neglected and poor.

Like the Children of Israel
in bondage to the King of Egypt,
we have the same standing:
   they call us only 'Jock'.

Our king after his crowning,
barely before he was adult,
turned into a poor stripped vagrant
   without guard or parliament or court.

Expelled from his rightful position
without any of his friends with him,
like a ship on the top of the ocean
   without rudder or oar or port.

I will go no more to Edinburgh
since Graham's blood was spilled there,
the lion valiant and mighty
   tortured on the gallows tree.

B'e sud am fìor dhuine uasal
Nach robh den linne shuarach,
Bu ro mhath rudhadh gruadhach
'N àm tarraing suas gu troid.

Deud chailc bu ro mhath dlùthadh
Fo mhala chaoil gun mhùgaich,
Ge tric do dhàil gam dhùsgadh
Cha rùisg mi chàch e nochd.

Mhic Nèill à Asaint chianail,
Nan glacainn an mo lìon thu
Bhiodh m'fhacal air do bhìnne
Is cha dìobrainn thu on chroich.

Thu fèin is t'athair cèile,
Fear taighe sin na Lèime,
Ged chrochta sibh le chèile
Cha b'èiric air mo lochd.

Craobh rùisgt' den abhall bhreugach
Gun mheas gun chliù gun cheutaidh
Bha riamh ri murt a chèile,
Nur fuidheall bheum is chorc.

Marbhaisg ort fèin, a dhìmheis,
Mar olc a reic thu an fhìrinn
Air son na mine Lìtich
Is dà thrian dith goirt.

XXVII. Do Mhac Leòid

Màiri nighean Alasdair Ruaidh

We have a good deal of oral tradition, but few facts, about Màiri nighean Alasdair Ruaidh. Perhaps born in Harris about 1615, in a family related to the MacLeods of Dunvegan (Sìol Tormaid), she is said to have become a nurse at Dunvegan and to have died after 1705. In that year Sir Tormod MacLeod of Berneray died, and we have her

He was a nobleman truly
of no paltry lineage,
his cheek's flushing was prodigious
   when drawing up to fight.

Chalk-white teeth set closely
under a slim unfrowning eye-brow,
though often your lot kept me wakeful
   I will not make it public tonight.

Son of Niall from dismal Assynt,
if in my net I could but trap you,
I would not banish you from the gallows,
   my word would seal your doom.

You yourself and your wife's father,
that house-holder of Lemlair,
even were you hanged together
   that would not compensate my loss.

Of the perjured apple-tree a bare offshoot
without fruit or fame or decorum
you were forever murdering each other,
   the left-overs of knives and blows.

A curse on you, you disgraced one,
for wickedly have you sold justice
for the sake of a boll of Leith-meal
   with two thirds of it gone sour.

XXVII. To MacLeod

*elegy for him: indeed, to judge from her extant verse it may be that she
was more closely associated with Berneray than with Dunvegan. This
song laments the death of one of the four MacLeod chiefs who died
during her career, but we have no way of telling which: Iain Mòr, 14th
of Dunvegan (d. 1649), brother of Sir Tormod of Berneray; Iain Mòr's
son Ruaidhri Sgaiteach, 15th (d. 1664); Ruaidhri's brother Iain
Breac, 16th (d. 1693); and Iain Breac's son Ruaidhri, 17th (d. 1699).
But this last Ruaidhri is the least likely, for there are indications that
Màiri, like An Clàrsair Dall (in no. XLI), severely disapproved of
his lifestyle.*

'S mòr mo mhulad 's mo phràmhan
'S mi gun mhacnas gun mhànran
Anns an talla am bu ghnàth le Mac Leòid.

Taigh mòr macnasach meadhrach
Nam macaomh 's nam maighdean
Far 'm bu tartarach gleadhraich nan còrn.

Tha do thalla mòr prìseil
Gun fhasgadh gun dìon ann,
Far am faca mi fion bhith ga òl,

Aig oighre Shìol Tormaid:
Fear th'eugais chan eòl damh –
Chan i an fhoill a chuir as duit no an stròdh.

Cuid dha t'àbhaist 's dha d' bheusan
A bhith gu fuilteach tric bèin-dearg
Air chuideachda chèir-gheal nan cròc.

Leat bu mhiann na coin lùthmhor
Dhol a shiubhal nan stùc-bheann,
Is an gunna nach diùltadh re òrd.

'S i do làmh nach robh tuisleach
Dhol a chaitheamh a' chuspair
Le d' bhogha cruaidh ruiteach deagh-neòil.

Great my dule and dolour
without dalliance or sporting
in the hall that was MacLeod's wonted haunt.

Great joyful blythe castle
of youths and of maidens
where drinking-horns' clatter was loud.

Your brilliant big building
without walls or roof timbers,
where I used to see wine being drunk,

By the heir of Tormod's descendants:
I know no man who bears resemblance –
neither dissoluteness nor deceit left you dead.

A part of your pastime and custom,
often your hide blood-spluttered,
was with the antlered white-buttocked throng.

You loved the lithe deerhounds
roaming the peaked hills
with the gun that always yielded to its lock.

Your hand would not falter
taking aim at the target
with your bow, ruddy and hard of good hue.

Bhiodh glac throm air do shliasaid
'S i gun ghaiseadh gun fhiaradh,
Bàrr dosrach de sgiathaibh an eòin.

Bhiodh cèir air do chrannaibh
Bu neo-èisleineach tarraing
Nuair a leumadh an tafaid bho ur meòir.

Nuair a leigteadh o d' làimh i
Cha bhiodh aon mhìr gun bhàthadh
Eadar corran a gàinne is a smeòirn.

'S ann sa' chlachan so shìos uam
Tha mo chàirdean 's mo dhìslean:
Ciamar thèid mi nam fianais aig bròn?

'S ann na luighe as-teampall
Tha m'aighear is m'annsachd:
Chaoidh cha tèid mi fhèin ann 's gun thu beò.

XXVIII. Fuaim an Taibh

Màiri nighean Alasdair Ruaidh

This song is addressed to Sir Tormod MacLeod of Berneray (c. 1614–1705) and dates from after his marriage in 1666(?) to Catrìona, daughter of Sir Seumas Mòr, MacDonald of Sleat, whose seat was Dùn Tuilm in Trotternish, Skye. It is clear from the opening stanzas that the poet was away from Sir Tormod at the time of composition, and it was doubtless composed during her exile: one of the few clear facts about her life is that she spent some time in exile from the MacLeod lands, the evidence consisting of both her songs and tradition. It is not at all certain why she was in exile, or where or when or for how long, but one of the songs composed during the exile certainly dates from after 1674.

Re fuaim an taibh
'S uaigneach mo ghean –
Bha mis uair nach b'e sean m'àbhaist,

On your thigh a heavy quiver,
arrows without twist or defect,
plumed tips of the wings of the fowl.

Your shafts sealed with beeswax
were not sluggish in bending
when the bowstring would leap from your hold.

When it was released from your fingers
no length would be unburied
between its pointed tip and its notch.

Below me in this graveyard
are my friends and relations:
what way can I draw near them in such woe?

Lying in the temple
is my joy and my treasure:
No more will I enter as you have gone.

XXVIII. The Ocean's Sound

At the ocean's sound
my mood is forlorn –
not always has feeling thus been my custom.

Ach pìob nuallanach mhòr
Bheireadh buaidh air gach ceòl
Nuair ghluaiste i le meòir Phàdraig.

Gur mairg a bheir gèill
Don t-saoghal gu lèir:
'S tric a chaochail e cheum gàbhaidh.

Gur lìonmhoire a chùrs
Na an dealt air an driùchd
Ann am madainn an tùs Màighe.

Chan fhacas rem' rè
Aon duine fui'n ghrèin
Nach tug e ghreis fèin dhà sin.

Thoir an t-soraidh so uam
Gu talla nan cuach
Far am biodh tathaich nan truagh dàimheil;

Thun an taighe nach gann
Fui'n leathad ud thall
Far bheil aighear is ceann mo mhànrain.

Shir Tormoid mo rùin,
Olgharach thù,
Foirmeil o thùs t'àbhaist.

A thasgaidh 's a chiall,
'S e bu chleachdadh duit riamh
Teach farsaing 's e fial fàilteach.

Bhiodh teanal nan cliar
Rè tamaill is cian
Dh'fhios a' bhaile am biodh triall chàirdean.

Nàile, chonnairc mi uair
'S glan an lasadh bha ad ghruaidh
Fui ghruaig chleachdaich nan dual àr-bhuidh'.

But a great roaring pipe
that left all music behind
when it was stirred by Patrick's fingers.

Woe to him who trusts
entirely in the world:
its perilous course has it often altered.

More numerous its ways
than the beads of the dew
on a morning in May's beginning.

All my days below the sun
I never saw the one
who was not given his turn of sorrow.

Bear this greeting from me
to the hall of the cups
where kinsfolk in distress would seek comfort.

To the house that goes not short
under yonder slope
where is joy and the subject of my crooning.

Sir Tormod my love,
one of Olghar's blood,
your custom of old, resplendent.

O treasure and dear,
it was ever your way
to keep a generous and ample household.

For months and from afar
a congregation of poet bands,
would move towards the place where friends gathered.

Forsooth, I have seen the time
when your cheek would burn bright
under hair that hung in ringlets, golden-yellow.

Fear dìreach deas treun
Bu ro fhìrinneach beus
'S e gun mhìghean gun cheum tràilleil,

Den linnidh b'fheàrr buaidh
Tha sna crìochaibh man cuairt,
Clann fhìrinneach Ruairidh làn-Mhòir.

Chan eil cleachdainn mhic rìgh
Na gaisge na gnìomh
Nach eil pearsa mo ghaoil làn dheth;

Ann an trèine is an lùth,
Ann an ceudfaidh 's an cliù,
Ann am fèile is an gnùis nàire;

An gaisge is an gnìomh
'S ann am pailte neo-chrìon,
Ann am maise is am miann àillteachd;

Ann an cruadal 's an toil,
Ann am buaidh thoirt air sgoil,
Ann an uaisle gun chron càileachd.

Tuigsear nan teud,
Purpais gach sgèil,
Susbaint gach cèill nàdair.

Gum bu chubhaidh dhuit siod,
Mar a thubhairt iad riut:
Bu tu an t-ubhal thar mios àrd-chraoibh.

Leòdach mo rùin,
Seòrsa fhuair cliù:
Cha bu thòiseachadh ùr dhàibh Sir.

Bha fios cò sìbh
Ann an iomartas rìgh,
Nuair bu mhuladach strì Theàrlaich.

A man straight, strong and brave
of the most upright of ways
without surliness or slavish conduct.

Of the most virtuous of blood
in the lands all round
the righteous brood of mighty Ruairidh.

There exists no prince's way,
no valour or heroic act,
that my loved one's character is not full of;

In bravery and force,
in understanding and renown,
in generosity and in modest demeanour;

In action and in pluck,
in giving without grudge,
in handsomeness and alluring beauty;

In hardiness and in love,
in surpassing knowledge of books,
in nobility without blot in temper.

Fine judge of the harp,
of the import of every tale,
of the meaning of every natural portent.

Of you this was apt,
just as they said:
you were the topmost apple of the high-tree.

MacLeod my love,
of a sort who won renown:
for them, no new honour was knighthood.

It was known who you were
in the bustle round a king,
when Charles' hostilities were vexing.

Slàn Ghàidhil no Ghoill
Gun d'fhuaras oirbh foill
Dh'aon bhuaireadh dhe'n d'rinn bhur nàmhaid.

Lochlannaich threun
Toiseach bhur sgèil,
Sliochd solta bha air freumh Mhànais.

Thug Dia dhuit mar ghibht
Bhith gu mòrdhalach glic;
Chrìosd deònaich dhad' shliochd bhith àghmhor.

Fhuair thu fortan o Dhia,
Bean bu shocraiche ciall
'S i gu foistinneach fial nàrach,

A bheil eineach is cliù
Is i gun mhilleadh no cùis,
'S i gu h-iriosal ciùin càirdeil;

I gun dolaidh fui'n ghrèin
Gu toileachadh treud
'S a folachd a rèir banrigh'n.

'S tric a riaraich thu cuilm
Gun fhiabhras gun tuilg:
Nighean oighre Dhùn Tuilm, slàn dhuit.

XXIX. Oran do Mhac Mhic Raghnaill na Ceapaich

Iain Lom

This song, as other versions make more obvious, is one of the group which Iain Lom composed in the wake of the Keppoch Murder of 1663. On 25 September in that year Raghnall, chief of the MacDonalds of Keppoch, and his brother Alasdair were murdered by members of their own clan, and Iain Lom seems to have been almost alone in his

I defy any Lowlander or Gael
to prove you guilty of false play
despite your enemies' temptations freely offered.

Norsemen bold,
the start of your account,
vigorous race of the stock of Manas.

God gave you the gift
of being magnificent and wise;
Christ, grant that your line may prosper.

You were granted a boon from God,
a most sensible spouse,
serene, modest and giving,

who has honour and fame
without blemish in her ways,
she is humble, sedate and friendly;

She is not lacking at all
in giving pleasure to flocks,
her blood in accordance with a princess.

Often have you served a feast
without frenzy or fuss:
daughter of Duntulm's heir, I hail you.

XXIX. A Song for MacDonald of Keppoch

*campaign to have the murderers brought to justice. He was opposed by
many of his kinsfolk and was at one point exiled to Kintail. But he
persisted and some of the guilty were beheaded in December 1665. In
this version, however, we have little more than a lament for the dead
chief.*

Mi am shuidhe air bhruaich torrain
Mun cuairt do Choire na Clèibhe,

Gar nach eil mo chas crùbach
Tha lot nas mù orm fo m' lèinidh.

Gar nach eil mo bhian sracte
Tha fo m'aisne mo chreuchdan;

'S chan e cùram na h-imrich
Na iomgain na sprèidhe,

Na bhith gam chur do Cheann Tàile
'S gun fhios cia an t-àite d'an tèid mi,

Ach bhith nochd gun cheann cinnidh –
'S tric 's gur minig leam fhèin sud –

Ceann cinnidh nam Bràighdeach
Chuireadh sgàth air luchd Beurla.

Cha b'e fuaim do ghreigh lodain
Gheibhte sodraich gu fèilltean,

Na geum do bha tomain
Dhol an coinneadh a ceud-laoigh,

Na uisge nan sluasaid
Far druabras na fèithe.

'S beag an t-iongnadh leam t'uaisle
Thighinn an uachdar air t'fheudail,

I am sitting on the side of a hillock
near to Coire na Clèibhe;

Though my leg is not crippled
beneath my shirt is greater maiming.

Though my skin is not ruptured
within my ribs are my woundings;

And it is not the anxiety over flitting
or concern about the cattle,

Or that to Kintail I am being exiled,
not knowing where I will go there,

But being tonight without chieftain –
oft and again that has been my portion –

The chief of the Braes of Lochaber
who struck fear into English speakers.

It was not your horses from the marshland
that would be heard trotting to the markets,

Nor your cow from the hill lowing
as she went to meet her first-born,

Nor water dripping from the shovels
with the sludge of the moorland.

Little my wonder your high birth
is apparent in your possessions,

'S a liuthad sruth uaibhreach
As 'n do bhuaineadh thu an ceud là.

Ceist nam fear thu on Fhearsaid
'S o Cheapach nam peuran,

'S o cheann Dail na Mine
Gu Sròn na h-Iolaire Lèithe:

'S e bu mhiann le d' luchd taighe
Bhith gan tathaich le beusan,

Mu dhà thaobh Gharbh a' Chonnaidh
Far 'm biodh na sonnanaich glè mhòr,

Le am morgha geur sgaiteach
Frith-bhacach garbh leumnach.

Tha mo choill air a maoladh,
Nì shaoil leam nach èireadh.

Tha mo chnothan air faoisgneadh
'S cha bu chaoch iad ri'm feuchainn,

'S nach eil agam dhiubh tuaileas –
Dh'fhuirich iad uam am bàrr gheugan.

XXX. Iorram na Sgiobaireachd

Murchadh Mòr mac mhic Mhurchaidh

Murchadh Mòr (d.c.1689) was the fifth MacKenzie of Achilty, near Contin in Easter Ross. He lived for a considerable time in Lewis, where his family had residences on Eilean Chalum Cille (in Loch Erisort) and in Stornoway, and were factors for the Earl of Seaforth. The poet was a notable seafarer, and the present song has been dated to around 1670, after he had left Lewis and was now evidently dependent on horse-transport. The musician mentioned in the last verse has been identified as Iain mac Mhurchaidh mhic Ailein (c.1630–1708), Morrison of Bragar, father of An Clàrsair Dall.

When you were plucked at the beginning
from so many proud blood-streams.

You are the darling of the men from Fearsaid
and from Keppoch of the pear-trees,

and from the head of Dail na Mine
to Sròn na h-Iolaire Lèithe:

The people of your household
liked to accomplish deeds of prowess,

About both sides of Garbh a' Chonnaidh
where the heroes were splendid,

With their sharp, jabbing javelins
barbed, stout and bounding.

My wood has been denuded,
something I thought would not happen.

My nuts have burst open
and they had not been found hollow.

And I have no way to impugn them –
they stayed out of my reach on branch-tips.

XXX. Song of Seafaring

Very Slow

Gur neo-shocrach mo cheum
Air chapall nan leum:
'S cha fhreagrar leat m'fheum air chòir.

Cha ghiùlain i an cèin
Ach aon duine is i fèin
Is gun cuireadh i feum air lòn.

Cha b'ionann 's mo làir
Air linnidh nam bàrc:
Bhiodh do ghillean do ghnàth cur bhòd.

Iùbhrach shocrach a' chuain
D'an cliù toiseach dol suas,
Giuthas dosrach nam buadh fo sheòl.

Buaidh 's beannachd don t-saor
Dh'fhuaigh a darach gu caoin,
'S i gun ghaiseadh gun ghaoid na bòrd.

Reubadh mara gu dlùth
O bheul sgar agus sùidh,
'N dèidh's a barradh gu h-ùr on òrd.

Ruithe choip air a blàr
Is i druidte gu h-àrd,
'S gum bu chruit leam a gàir fo sheòl.

O aigeal nan gleann
Gu baideal nam beann
Bhiodh sadan is deann mu sròin.

Siod i agam, mo shaoidh,
'S i na ruith air a' ghaoith
Gun bhioraibh ri taoibh 's i folbh.

'S nuair a ghabhamaid mu thàmh
Ann an calaphort shèimh
Cha b'fhallain fo ar làimh na ròin.

Unsteady my pace
on the bounding mare:
my need you do not answer at all.

No distance will she bear
any but one man and herself
and for that she'd be in need of mash.

Not so my mare
on the channel of barks:
your youths were always waging stakes.

Smooth ship of the flood,
famed of rising prow,
dense pine of powers under sail.

Strength and health to the wright
who pegged her timber tight,
without blemish or blight in her planks.

Cleaving the ocean clean,
from edge of scarf and seam,
with her rivetting sealed by the mall.

On her outsides streaming foam,
up high her rigging soaked,
harp music to me her shout under sail.

From the troughs of the glens
to the crests of the bens
there'd be foam and ferment round her prow.

Yon mare is my delight,
as she runs before the wind,
with no spurs in her sides as she moves.

And when we'd come to halt
in a peaceful bay
the seals would not be safe in our hands.

Bhiodh ar sgeanan glè gheur
Gu feannadh an fhèidh
'S cha b'annas an gleus ud oirnn.

Bhiodh saill an daimh mhodhair
Fo ar n-àilgheas 's fo ar roghainn,
'S e air fàgail a laoigh sa' cheò.

Sin is eilid nam beann
Nach teàrnadh gu gleann
Gun cheilearan teann na lorg.

B'i siod m'aighear 's mo mhiann,
Gad a ghlas air mo chiabh,
'S cha b'e an t-slatag no an t-srian bhith 'm dhòrn.

Fhir a dh'imcheas an iar,
Bho nach cinnteach mo thriall,
Bi ag innse gur bliadhn gach lò.

Thoir mo shoraidh a nunn
A dh'ionnsaigh an fhuinn
Far am faighte na suinn ag òl;

Luchd lùireach is lann
Chuireadh cùl ri bhith gann
'S a bhiodh cliùiteach an àm an òil,

Gun àrdan gun strì,
Gun àireamh air nì,
Gun sàradh air fion no beòir;

Ceòil fidhle nar cluais
On Eòin fhìnealta shuairc
O'm bu mhisle cur dhuan air folbh.

Our knives were kept keen
for skinning the deer,
no rarity was that deed to us.

The limber buck's fat
was our choice of feast
after leaving his calf in the fog.

That, and the hind of the crags
who would not descend to the strath
were stalkers not hard in her tracks.

That mare would be my joy and my aim,
though my temples have grown grey,
and not the goad or the reins in my palms.

O man who travels west,
since uncertain my way,
tell that every day seems a year.

Carry my greeting across
towards the lands
where the drinking warriors were found;

People of breast-plates and swords,
who rejected going short
and whose times of carousing were renowned,

Without pride or strife,
without assessing the price,
without restraint in wine or ale;

Fiddle music in our ears,
from gentle nimble Eoin
who was sweetest at sending forth an air.

XXXI. Is Garbh a-nochd an Oidhch' rim' Thaobh

Murchadh Mòr mac mhic Mhurchaidh

A tradition given with this song in the manuscript which is its only source says that Murchadh 'was at a wedding in the Island of Lewis, then a widower, and being urged upon by some friends to marry a second time, he composed the following song making a ship a comparison between his late and future spouse.' Metrically the song shows signs of having originated in (loose) syllabic quatrains, of a type used by Murchadh in some of his poems in the Fernaig manuscript, and then having come into the oral tradition in a form based on a version of our no. XXV.

Is garbh a-nochd an oidhch' rim' thaobh,
　　a chailin òig, nach stiùir thu i,
tha loingeas aig càch fo sheòl,
　　a chailin òig, nach stiùir thu i;
's tha mise fo bhròn gun fhonn
bhon chaill mi m'eithear fo sheòl:
an ochdramhach a b'fhasa rian
gun àrdan gun strì gun chàs,
an iubhrach bhuaidheach ghàirdeil chuimir,
curach suairc on bhuinne mhear,
cobhar criosgheal na crann duilleach,
bròn briste nan iomair,
rachadh na grinneach a-suas
gun beantainn ri cruas na h-aon:
's minic a shiubhlainn an sàl
lem' iubhraich bhig bhàin gun ghaoth.

XXXI. Rough is the Night without

Rough is the night without,
   O young maid, won't you take her helm,
the other's ships are under sail,
   O young maid, won't you take her helm;
and I am downcast without cheer
as I lost my galley under sail;
the smoothest-sailing, eight-oared boat,
without haughtiness, trouble or strife,
the shapely triumphant glad yew,
gentle coracle from the lively stream,
a foam circlet in her leafy mast,
the travail of breaking the lea,
like a stripling she'd rise up
not cleaving rigidly to one:
often did I sail the brine
with my fair little skiff and no wind.

Cha tèid mi dham' dheòin gu muir,
sguiridh mi thathaich a' chuain;
cha stiùirear leam stuagh no tuil
bhristeadh le foirneart gun ghaoith.
'S misde mi a chaoidh a cor:
chan àil leam sgùda gun tlachd,
chan àil leam bàrca gun dìon
's chan àil leam corrbhinneach ùr
nach seòladh le triùir 's mi fhìn.
Clàraibh corrach is i crìon
cha b'i mo mhiann sa' mhuir chas,
'n àm iomain nan stuagh 's i brais,
nach fuiligeadh tional an t-sluaigh
ach sgapadh a-tuath 's a-deas
cumha na luinge tha bhuam
dha nach d'fhuaras riamh bonn lochd:
's mo chridhe tha garbh a-nochd.

XXXII. Marbhrainn do Mhac Gille Chaluim Ratharsaidh

Iain Garbh, 6th MacLeod of Raasay (Mac Gille Chaluim), was drowned at Easter (23rd April) 1671, when his ship sank in a storm on the way home from a christening feast at the Lewis home of Coinneach Mòr, 3rd Earl of Seaforth. Iain Garbh was an exceptionally strong and handsome man, and it is said that one of his sisters composed a lament for him every Friday for a year after his death. We have five extant laments, ascribed to various poets.

> *O hiò rò bhì is gun thu thighinn fallain,*
> *O hiò rò bhì ì rù bhi hu ag thall,*
> *S no hiò rò bhì is gun thu thighinn fallain.*

Seall a-mach an e an latha e
'S mi feitheamh na fàire:
'S e an sgeula nach binn leam
Chuaidh innseadh o Chàisg dhamh.

S no hiò rò bhì is gun thu thighinn fallain.

Not willingly will I go to sea,
I'll crave the ocean no more;
I'll sail neither billow nor flood
that could destroy by force without wind.
I'm the worse evermore for her state:
I desire no virtueless ketch,
I want no bark unsound
nor new, long-sheeted boat
that would not take three and myself.
A warped skiff of wobbly planks
not her my wish on rough seas,
when the waves would drive her fast,
and she couldn't bear the number of crew,
but floundering north and south
in return for the ship I've lost
in whom was never found fault:
it is my heart that tonight is rough.

XXXII. Elegy for Mac Gille Chaluim of Raasay

O hiò rò bhì is gun thu thighinn fall-ain, O hiò rò bhì l rù bhi hu ag thall, S no hiò ro bhì is gun thu thighinn fall-ain. Seall a-mach an e an lath-a e 'S mi feith-eamh na fàir-e: 'S e an sgeul-a nach binn leam Chuaidh. inns-eadh o Chàisg dhamh. S no hiò rò bhì is gun thu thighinn fall-ain.

Look out if it is dawn yet,
as I wait for daybreak:
Tidings that were not pleasing
were told me at Easter.

O hiò rò bhì
Since you did not come safely.

'S e an sgeula nach binn leam
Chuaidh innseadh o Chàisg dhamh:
T'fhaotainn bàite air a' charragh
Mar re Calum do bhràthair.

Fear mòr thu Shìol Torcaill –
'S e do chorp a bha làidir.

O is maith thig dhuit breacan
Air a lasadh le càrnaid,

'S cha mheas thig dhuit triubhas,
Dol a shiubhal nan sràidean.

Nochd is mòr tha dhe t'iargain
Air Iarla Cheann Tàile,

Nach raibh 'n soirbheas ud rèidh dhuit
'S gur tu fhèin air a b'àirde.

Dìreadh muigh ris an rubha,
Fhuair sibh 'n sgiùrsadh nach b'àil leam;

Bha sibh salach le siaban
Tigh'nn o lèantanaibh bàite.

Dh'fhàg e smuainean air m'aignidh
Dh'fhàg gun chadal ochd tràth mi,

Mheud 's a gheabhainn do bheadradh
Nuair a thiginn gu t'àras.

'S maith thig sud os cionn t'fhèile ort,
Claidheamh geur nan lann Spàinneach,

Mar re duille air a cèireadh
'S sgiath rèidh air do cheàrr-laimh.

Tidings that were not pleasing
were told me at Easter:
Of finding you drowned on the rock-slab
along with Calum your brother.

A big man of the seed of Torcall –
powerful was your body.

It is well you suit tartan,
lit up with scarlet,

No less do trews become you,
as you travel the causeways.

Tonight you are sore regretted
by the Earl of Kintail,

That fair wind was not constant
when you were running with it highest.

Climbing out by the headland
you got the mangling I hated;

You were sullied with spindrift
coming from the drowned meadows.

It left thoughts on my spirit
that left me eight nights sleepless,

Of all the affection I was given
when I came to your dwelling.

Over your kilt these suit you:
a sharp sword, Spanish-bladed,

With waxed scabbard
and shield set on your left arm.

Làmh dheas air a' chuspair,
Cha b'ann bharr uchdan nan gàrlach.

'S ged a thigeadh iad uile
Bu leat urram nan Gàidheal.

XXXIII. Moladh na Pìoba

Gilleasbaig na Ceapaich

Gilleasbaig was chief of the MacDonalds of Keppoch from about 1670 till his death in 1682; he was a fairly productive poet, and father of Sìleas na Ceapaich (c. 1660–c. 1729). We do not know when he composed this poem, but it is apparently a response to one attacking the pipes made long before by Niall Mòr MacMhuirich, who also composed our no. VII. In defence of the pipes, Gilleasbaig compares them favourably with dàn *(poetry), which was Niall Mòr's skill. Gilleasbaig's poem was the spur to two later Maclean songs, one supporting his view of the pipes and the other against it.*

'S mairg do dhi-moil ceòl is caismeachd,
    Prosnadh slòigh go gaisgeachd threun;
Mòr phìob leis an dùisgear gach misneach,
    A torman mòid is misde beum.

Mo ghaol clàirseach, ro ghaol pìob,
    Mì-thlachd leam an tì do chàin;
Olc an duais aig ceòl droch-comain,
    Bonn-chluas aig ollamh ri dàn.

Cha bhi mi di-moladh an dàin
    Ach 's ann bu mhaith an dàn san t-sìth;
Air a nàmhaid cha deachaidh an dàn
    Riamh cho dàna is a chuaidh ì.

Nam faiceadh tu fir air learg
    Fui mheirge am bi dearg is bàn,
B'fheàrr leam spealtadh dhith ri h-uair
    Na na bhuil go tuaim de dhàn.

A good hand at the target,
not from the tunic of the urchins.

And even were all gathered
yours the Gaels' honour.

XXXIII. The Praise of the Bagpipes

Woe to the one who decries music and war-march,
  to mighty heroism inciting hosts;
great pipe that inspires all courage
  her noise, the more terrible for its beat.

I love the harp, my great love the pipe,
  I abominate the one who it decries;
no sense of obligation is poor reward for music,
  the deaf ear of a poet busy with verse.

I am not about to dispraise verse,
  for verse would be all right at time of peace;
but verse never affected her foes
  anything as deeply as did the pipe.

If you were to see men on a slope
  under a banner of red and white,
better a blast from the pipe for an hour
  than all the poetry between here and the grave.

Bu bhinn leam torman a dos
  'S i cruinneachadh arm fo sgiort:
An dàn nan tigeadh fo brat
  Gu ceart gum b'fheàrr lè bhith 'n Hiort!

Bhean bhinn-fhoclach nach breun sturt,
  Chiùin chaoin-fhoclach, 's nìor breug sin,
Labhras go sèimh air gach modh
  'S a brèid air slinneanaibh fir.

An crann 's mò chruinnich na slòigh,
Ga dhi-moladh fa dheòidh is mairg.

                    'S mairg do dhi-moil.

XXXIV. Biodh an Uidheam seo Triall

Iain Lom

*There are several versions of this song, but it is not clear from any of
them who the subject is, or what was the occasion of the song. On the
evidence of our version alone, it could be addressed to Dòmhnall a'
Chogaidh (d.1718), before he became the 11th MacDonald of Sleat
in 1695. His father, Sir Dòmhnall, 10th, would then have been alive,
and may be mentioned in the 8th verse.*

Biodh an uidheam seo triall
Gu ceann uidhe nan cliar
Far 'm bu chubhaidh 's bu mhiann le seòid;

Gu tùr meadhrach nach crìon
Nan ceann còmhraidh 's glan fiamh,
Cùirt ghreadhnach bhon rìoghail stoirm;

Gu àras mo rùin
'N cluinnte clàrsaichean ciùil,
Iomairt thàilisg air chrùntaibh òir.

Sweet to me the sound of her drones
    gathering armies under her skirts:
if a poem chanced to come under her cloak
    she would feel better off in Hiort!

The sweet-worded woman with never a rotten huff,
    gentle smooth-worded, and that is no lie,
who speaks softly in every mode,
    on a man's shoulders her kerchief thrown.

The standard greatest for rallying hosts,
    to decry it finally is woe.

                Woe to the one who decries.

XXXIV. Let this song make its way

Let this song make its way
to the poets' journey's end
that heroes used rightly to long for;

To a merry fort that knows no stint,
of the handsome folk most talked about,
splendid court from which spreads a royal stir;

To the hall of my love
where harps' music was heard,
gambling at the gammon for crowns of gold.

Bhiodh mnài àille an fhuilt rèidh
Gabhail dàna le teud,
Sìor chur seachad na sèisteachd leò.

Bheir mi an ruathar seo nunn
Shealltainn oighre Dhùn Tuilm:
Gum meal thu an stoidhleadh bho thùs rid' bheò.

Iuchair ghliocas nach bàth
Cur a radhairc thar chàch:
'S tu gun taghainn den àl-s' tha beò.

Mach bho mhorair nan steud
Le an cluinnte orghan nan teud,
'S tu b'fhoirmeile beus tràth-nòin.

'S leat Sir Dòmhnall bhon Chaol,
'S leat Clann Dòmhnaill nan laoch,
Sud a' bhuidheann nach maom san tòir.

'S leat Mac Mhic Ailein bhon chuan
Le loingeas daraich lom luath:
Luchd nan leadan bho am buailte stròic.

'S leat Mac Mhic Alasdair fhèil
Bho Ghlinn Garadh nan geug,
Buidheann bharrail nach gèill fo ur sgòd.

'S leat fir Eireann a-rìst,
Chuir thu fhèin air do thì:
'S iad gun èireadh le strì mud' dhòrn.

Gur leat urram gach seilg
Led' cheòl druma ga sheinn
Roimh d' gheàrd Muileach nach meirbh san tòir.

Macail màidsearail ùr
Faicheil eireachdail ciùin,
Marcaich greadhnach nan cruidh-each gorm.

The lovely women of smooth hair,
singing song to the harp,
giving out the chorus time and again.

I will make a rush across
to visit Duntulm's heir:
may you enjoy the title all the days of your life.

Key of wisdom not vain,
of vision beyond the rest:
of all the living it is you I would choose.

Apart from the lord of the steeds
with whom was heard the organ of strings,
yours was the most impressive of music at night.

With you stands Sir Donald from Kyle,
and Clan Donald of the fighting men,
those are the company who do not panic in the chase.

With you, Mac Mhic Ailein from over the sea
with his quick lean ships of oak:
the long-tressed men from whom blows would rain down.

With you generous Mac Mhic Alasdair's son
from Glengarry of the trees,
an excelling group who in your command will not yield.

Yours the men of Ireland as well,
whom you mustered yourself:
they would gather about your fist for the fight.

You had the honour of every hunt,
your drum resounding at the head
of your Mull guard who are not weak in the pursuit.

Fond, commanding, young man,
dapper, handsome and calm,
magnificent rider of the shod, grey steeds.

Bhiodh eich sheanga nan leum
'S iad nan deannaibh cur rèis,
Fir a' sreamadh na srèin r'am beòil.

XXXV. Luinneag Mhic Neachdainn

This is a song of praise to a MacNaughton chief, but it is hard to be sure which one. Trying to reconcile apparently contradictory internal evidence, we have concluded that the most likely candidate is Colonel Alasdair MacNaughton of Dùn dà Ràmh (Dundarave etc.), near Inveraray on Loch Fyne, head of his clan and son of Malcolm MacNaughton of Glenshira (d.c.1647) and Elizabeth Murray. Between 1651 and 1653 Alasdair acted as the Earl of Argyll's chamberlain in Kintyre, and he seems to have died around 1685. In stanza 4 the poet gives attention to his links with the Campbells (represented by the personal name Duibhne) and the MacDonalds (Colla, and probably Seumas). There seems to be an especially strong link between MacNaughton and the (MacDonald) Earls of Antrim, for one Sèan Dubh MacNeachdainn (d.c.1630) is said to have been 'secretarius' to Somhairle Buidhe, father of the first Earl of Antrim: a direct genealogical link between Alasdair and Sèan Dubh has also been suggested. Since in stanza 12 Alasdair Dubh of Glengarry (d.1721) is named as one of the subject's (potential) allies, the song will probably have to be dated to the period 1680–1685. Alasdair Dubh was the effective leader of his clan in 1689: perhaps this song can be taken as evidence that he was already the effective leader by 1685.

'S fhad tha mi ag èisdeachd ri ur dìochuimhn,
A' cur air tuireamh gu lìonmhor
Air clann nam bodachana crìona
Gun luaidh air uaislean na tìre.
Maighistir an fhuinn so shìos uainn,
An Leitir bheag is an Dùn prìseil,
Ceist nam ban on Chlachan Shìorach.

Slender leaping steeds
would be racing at full speed,
with men curbing the reins round their mouths.

XXXV. Mac Neachdainn's Song

Long have I listened to your oblivious ramblings
as you pile on copious praise in mourning
the offspring of silly old bauchles
with not a word of the country's nobles.
The lord of this land that lies below us,
little Leitir and the Dùn splendid,
the darling of the women of Clachan Sìorach.

Hó hì hiù rubh ò, hì hó ruinn ó,
Hì hiù rubh ó, hì hó riunn ò,
Hì hiù rubh ó, hì hó riunn ó,
Hì hiù rubh ó, hì hóg i hò.

Ge b'e thagradh ann an strì ort,
Gu dearbh cha b'fhada gun dol sìos e.
Dh'èireadh Gòrdanaich leat dìleas,
Luchd nan trupa gorma cruidheach;
'S lìonmhor aca pasgan phìcean,
'S lìonmhor brataichean is pìoban,
'S lìonmhor clogaid is cuilìobhair,
'S lìonmhor bogha is saighead dhìreach,
'S lìonmhor dag is sgithean phrìseil,
'S lìonmhor spàinteach air thaobh clì orr,
Glac an iubhair ann am bian-ghlaic.

Ge b'e thagradh ort gun reusan,
Bu cham a' chòmhdhail da nuair dh'èireadh.
Thig iomadh connspann leat à Eirinn:
Thig Iarl Anndram nan each ceumnach
Bheir a bhàrcan is còig ceud leis;
'S iomadh curaidh calma treubhach
Thig à Ile ort nan dèidh sud:
Thig Luing is Saoil an adhbhar t'fheirge.

Chan iongnadh dhuit-se bhith èibhinn:
'S iomadh sruthan bras fod' lèinidh
De shìol nan curaidhne gleusda:
Car thu Dhuibhne, Cholla, Sheumas,
Shomhairle Bhuidhe nan geur-lann
'S do Dhòmhnall Gorm a bha an Slèite;
Car thu Dhonnchadh Ruadh na Fèile.

Chuir mi iùl ort, is cha b'aithreach,
'N tùs an t-samhraidh so chaidh thairis,
Air òg finealta dh'fhàs barrail;
Bha thu càirdeach do Mhac Cailein,
Do Dhùn Olla nan stuagh geala;
Car thu Thighearna Loch nan Eala,
Do Dhonnchadh Diùrach 's do dh'Ailein.

Whosoever met with you in conflict,
indeed he was soon defeated.
With you Gordons would rise faithful,
the troops with the shod, grey horses;
numerous their pikes in bundles,
numerous their pipes and banners,
numerous their guns and helmets,
numerous their bows and straight arrows,
numerous their precious dirks and pistols,
numerous the toledos at their left-sides,
in a quiver of yew in a hide cover.

Whosoever would accuse you without reason,
rough on him the tryst when it happened.
Many a hero will rise with you from Ireland:
the Earl of Antrim of the stepping horses
will bring his ships and five hundred;
many a resolute mighty champion
from Islay too will come to join you:
Luing and Seil will rise in the cause of your anger.

It was no wonder that you were comely:
with many fast streams beneath your linen
of the seed of the skilful champions:
you are a relation of Duibhne, Colla, Seumas,
of Somhairle Buidhe of sharp sword-blades
and of Dòmhnall Gorm who was in Slèite;
of Donnchadh Ruadh na Fèile.

I came to know you, no disappointment,
at the beginning of this summer just over,
the refined young man who has grown up superbly;
you were related to Mac Cailein,
to Dunollie of the white billows,
a relation of the Lord of Loch nan Eala,
of Donnchadh of Jura and of Ailean.

Is ionmhainn leam Iain as òige,
Calpa deas air thùs na tòrach;
'S math thig lùireach dhuit is gòirseid
Agus lèine 'n anart Hòlaind,
Còta goirid air a òradh
'S boineid bhreac nan caitein gorma
'S breacan nan triuchana bòidheach.

Alasdair a' chùlain chleachdaich,
Sud am beus a gheibhte ad chaisteal:
Bhith 'g òl fiona is cluich air chairtean,
Do cheathairne òg eutrom ghasda
Ag òl air uaislean 's ga chur seachad
A pìosaibh òir air an lasadh.

Alasdair a' chùlain bhuidhe,
Gun robh 'n Rìgh dhuit mar mo ghuidhe.
Ceist nam ban on Ghleannan chumhann
'S on Leitir an cois an Rubha,
Slat is dìrich' thu at uidheam.

'S Neachdannach do shloinne dìreach
'S cha b'ann an cagar os n'ìosal;
Tha thu shliochd nam Moireacha prìseil
Dhèanadh luchd ealaidh a dhìoladh.

Oigear aigeantach gun àrdan,
Ceannard air feachd thu neo-chearbach,
Gàirdean geal dha'm math thig armachd;
'S math thig claidheamh dhuit is targaid
Agus stapall den òr dheallrach
'S pìc ùr a dh'iubhar na Meallraich
'S glac nan ceann sgaiteach on cheàrdaich.

Beloved to me Iain the younger,
a leg with fine calf at the forefront of battle;
well do you suit a cuirass and gorget
with a shirt made of linen from Holland,
a short coat with gold braiding,
the tartan bonnet with blue tail ribands
and the tartan plaid of stripes most handsome.

Alasdair of the clustering ringlets,
this the way of life found in your castle:
drinking of wine and card-playing,
your fighting bands, young, handsome, sprightly,
drinking to nobles and knocking it back from
cups of gold, brightly burnished.

Alasdair of the yellow tresses,
may the King treat you as I beseech Him.
The darling of the women from narrow Gleannan
and the women from Leitir beside the Headland,
the straightest of rods are you in armour.

Your direct descent is with the MacNaughtons
and that was not said in a low whisper;
you are of the line of precious Murrays
who gave poets payment in plenty.

Mettlesome youth devoid of hauteur,
leader of an army without a blemish,
white arm that looks good in armour;
well do you suit a sword and target
fixed with a staple of gold, gleaming,
a new bow made from the yew of Meallrach
and puncturing arrow-heads forged at the smithy.

'S lìonmhor claidheamh dh'èireadh leat-sa:
Thig Mac Raghnaill ort on Cheapaich,
Mac Iain Stiùbhart as an Apainn;
Thig Mac Dhòmhnaill Duibh on Chorpaich,
Thig Mac an Aba à Gleann Dochart
'S Tighearna Ghrannt o Bhaile Chaisteil;
Thig Mac Shimidh is Clann Chatain
'S Iarla Shìophort nan garbh bhratach.

Dh'èireadh sud leat ann ad chabhaig,
Alasdair Dubh Ghlinne Garaidh,
Triath na Lùib 's na Learga mar-ris
'S am Meinnearach gun ghaog mar charaid;
Ogha Dhonnchadh Duibh a' Bhealaich
Is Mac Phàrlain às an Arair
'S Mac Laghmainn o thaobh na mara.

Shaorainn Ealasaid o mhulad,
Ceist nam ban o thùr nan uinneag:
Gun glèidh an Rìgh do dhà chuilein
'S gun seachainn e uatha tubaist –
'S nam b'àill leibh e dhèanainn tuille.

XXXVI. Marbhrann Thighearna na Comraich

*Iain Molach succeeded as 2nd MacKenzie of Applecross on the death
of his father Ruaraidh in 1646, and died (at Easter) in 1684 or 1685.
His generosity, especially to visiting poets and harpers, was legendary
(and this song alludes to it), and we have a tradition telling how the
Earl of Antrim's harper carried Iain Molach's fame to Ireland.
Perhaps that is why this song is ascribed, in the only primary manu-
script source, to 'an Irish poet'.*

Many the swords that would rise to support you:
Mac Raghnaill will come to you from Keppoch,
Mac Iain of the Stewarts of Appin;
Mac Dhòmhnaill Dhuibh will come from Corpach,
Mac an Aba from Glen Dochart
and Lord Grant from Baile Chaisteil;
Mac Shimidh will come and Clan Chattan
and the Earl of Seaforth of the fierce banners.

These would rise with you in a hurry,
Alasdair Dubh of Glengarry,
the Lord of Lùb and Learg also
and Menzies without flaw as comrade;
the grandson of Donnchadh Dubh of Bealach
and Mac Phàrlain from Arair
and Mac Laghmainn from the coastline.

Would that I could spare Ealasaid from sorrow,
the paragon of women from the tower of windows:
may God preserve your two young ones
and may He shelter them from mishap –
and if it would please you, I could sing further.

XXXVI. Elegy to the Laird of Applecross

An taobh tuath ud cha tèid mi
Air chuairt no air chèilidh
Bho chualas gun d'eug thu,
Dheagh mhic Ruaraidh na fèile;
Liuthad airm agus èididh
Agus earraidh is eudail
Agus gleus dol air leughadh
A liubhair geal-ghlac na fèile
Do luchd falbha is do sgeulaiche beòil.

Leam a b'ait a bhith làmh riut
Dol air siubhal le bàta;
Bhitheadh buidheann mo ghràidh ann
A' cur a' ghiuthais gu sàile,
'S iad ga lughadh gu làidir
Ris na rubhachan àirde;
Gad a dhùisgeadh tuinn àrda
Chuireadh t'aogas fiamh gàire oirnn,
Gad bhiodh sruth is muir gàirthich ma sròin.

'S ann an earrach na Càsga
Bhuail gearan gu bràth mi
A chuir tost air mo chlàirsich,
Mu fhear baile na fàilte
Bha gu tighearnail pàirteil
Caomhail carthannach càirdeil
Mòr-urramach stàiteil:
'Se sgeula do bhàis
A thug air iomadh bhith fàisgeadh nan dòrn.

Dh'imich cliù ort an Albainn
Eadar Sealltainn 's a' Gharbhmach,
Mullach Srutha is Druim Farbairn
Is na h-eileine fairge:
Chuala Eirinn ort seanchas
'S bhiodh a bàrda gad leanmhainn:
Cha mhilleadh tu an t-ainm sin,
Fhir a bhuinnig 's a dhearbhe,
A làmh a liubhairt an airgid 's an òir.

No more will I head northwards,
neither on circuit nor to visit,
since I head you are departed,
good son of Ruaraidh of plenty;
so much weaponry and armour,
and clothing and treasure,
such readiness to study
has the good white hand granted
to travellers and to tellers of tales.

I delighted in being with you
going on a voyage in a galley;
the crew of my dear companions
putting the oars out on the oceans,
flexing them with vigour
against the high wave-crests;
when there arose rough billows
your face would reassure us
despite the current and churning seas round her prow.

It was in the spring at Easter
lasting grief struck me
that silenced my clàrsach
concerning the host of great welcome
who was lordly and partial,
tender, kind and friendly,
greatly honoured and stately:
it was the news of your passing
that has caused many to be wringing their hands.

Your fame has spread in Scotland
between Shetland and the Garbhmach,
Mullach Srutha and Druim Farbairn
and the sea-girt islands:
Ireland heard report of you
and her poets pursued you:
you could never spoil that reputation,
O man who won it and proved it,
O hand to bestow silver and gold.

Dh'fholbh Cailean Ruadh cliùtach
'S fear math taighe na Cùileadh,
Fear na Comraich air chùl sin,
Leòghann aigeannach cùirteil:
Dh'fhàg sud m'fheusag fo dhriùchdainn
Agus m'aigne neo-shùnntach
'Chionn nach urra mi d' dhùsgadh:
Bidh mi ad dhèidh gu bochd brùite rem' bheò.

A' chraobh thu b'àirde anns a' choille,
Thar gach preas bha thu soilleir,
A' cumail dìon air an doire
Le d' sgèimh ghuirm fo bhlàth dhuilleag;
Cha b'e mhàin Clanna Choinnich
Bhiodh mun cuairt dhuit ma Challainn,
Bhiodh gach fine agus sloinne
A' teachd le càirdeas ad choinneamh:
Bhiodh fir Eireann 's nan eilean mud' bhòrd.

XXXVII. Air dha bhith uair an Dùn Eideann

An Ciaran Mabach

Gilleasbaig Ruadh mac Mhic Dhòmhnaill, nicknamed An Ciaran Mabach, was brother of Sir Seumas Mòr (d. 1678; also called Seumas Ruadh), MacDonald of Sleat, and son of Dòmhnall Gorm Og, the subject of no. XIX, and Seònaid, the subject of no. XVIII. In 1654 he acquired land in Borghraidh na Sgiotaig in Trotternish, Skye, but he also held land in North Uist; he was living in Uist in 1665 when he acted for his brother in avenging the Keppoch murder (see no. XXIX), and he is said to have died in 1688. This song is said to have been composed during a time he spent in Edinburgh, attending doctors because of an injury to his leg: it might be argued on the basis of stanza 3 that this was not long before his death. Places in the west where he says (stanzas 2 and 3) that he would like to hunt again appear to include some in Skye, some in Lewis (owned by his MacKenzie cousins) and some in North Uist.

Famed Cailean Ruadh has departed
and the good host of Cùil's household,
The Laird of Applecross soon after,
a lion spirited and courteous:
that has left my spirit dejected
and my beard moist with tear-drops
for I cannot rouse you:
without you, I am forever wretched and bruised.

You were the highest tree in the forest,
over every thicket you stood distinctive,
affording shelter to the oakgrove
with your vigorous beauty under heavy foliage;
not only Clan MacKenzie
at New Year gathered round you,
for each tribe and lineage
came to see you with good wishes:
with men of Ireland and the islands about your board.

XXXVII. On his being once in Edinburgh

Ge socrach mo leaba
 B'annsa cadal air fraoch
Ann an lagan beag uaigneach
 Is bad den luachar rim' thaobh;
Nuair a dh'èirinn sa' mhadainn
 Bhith siubhal ghlacagan caol
Na bhith triall chun na h-Abaid,
 'G èisdeachd glagraich nan saor.

'S oil leam càradh na frìthe
 (Is mi bhith 'n Lìte nan long)
Eadar ceann Sàileas Sìphort
 'S rubha Ghrianaig nan tonn,
Agus Uiginnis riabhach,
 An tric an d'iarr mi damh donn
'S a bhith triall chun nam bodach
 Dh'am bu chosnadh cas chrom.

Chan eil agam cù gleusda
 Is chan eil feum agam dhà;
Cha suidh mi air baca
 Am monadh fada o chàch;
Cha leig mi mo ghadhar –
 Chaidh faghaid an t-Sròim Bàin –
'S cha sgaoil mi mo luaidh
 An Gleann Ruathain gu bràth.

B'iad mo ghràdh-sa a' ghreigh uallach
 A thogadh suas ris an àird,
Dh'itheadh biolair an fhuarain
 'S air 'm bu shuarach an càl;
'S mise fèin nach tug fuath dhuibh,
 Ged a b'fhuar am mìos Màigh –
'S tric a dh'fhulaing mi cruadal
 'S mòran fuachd air ur sgàth.

Though comfy my bolster
   I'd sooner sleep on the moor
in a lonely snug hollow,
   a clump of rush at my side;
when I'd rise in the mornings
   take the narrow defiles
rather than be making for the Abbey,
   deafened by joiners at work.

Vexing the thought of the moorland
   (while I'm in Leith of the ships)
between the head of Sàileas Sìphort
   and Grianaig point of the waves,
and Uiginnis lying dappled
   where often I brought down a brown stag,
instead I approach the old worthies
   who'd make a living from a gammy leg.

I have no trained deerhound
   and of one I've no use;
I'll sit on no peat-hag
   on a moor far from all;
I have no hound to send after –
   the Sròm Bàn hunt has dispersed –
and my lead I will scatter
   in Gleann Ruathain no more.

My love the proud deer-herds
   that would rise up by the point,
who ate cress from the fountain
   and on kale looked askance:
I bore them no ill-will,
   though chill the month of May –
often have I suffered discomfort
   and great cold for your sakes.

B'e mo ghràdh-sa am fear buidhe
  Nach suidheadh mun bhòrd,
Nach iarradh ri cheannach
  Pinnt leanna na beòir:
Uisge beatha math dùbailt
  Cha bu diù leat ri òl –
B'fheàrr leat biolair an fhuarain
  Is uisge luaineach an lòin.

B'i mo ghràdh-sa a' bhean uasal
  Dha nach d'fhuaras riamh lochd,
Nach iarradh mar chluasaig
  Ach fior ghualainn nan cnoc,
'S nach fuiligeadh an t-sradag
  A lasadh ri corp:
Och a Mhoire, mo chruaidh-chàs
  Nach d'fhuair mi thu nochd!

Bean a b'aigeantaich cèile
  An àm èirigh ri driùchd:
Chan fhaigheadh tu beud da
  Is cha bu lèir leis ach thù;
Sibh an glacaibh a chèile
  Am fior eudann nan stùc,
'S an àm èirigh na grèine
  Bu ghlan lèirsinn do shùl.

Nuair a thigeadh am foghar
  Bu mhiann leam gleadhar do chlèibh,
Dol a ghabhail a' chrònain
  Air a' mhòintich bhuig rèidh,
Dol an coinneamh do leannain
  Bu ghile feaman is cèir;
Gur i an eilid bu bhòidhche
  Is bu bhrisge lòghmhoire ceum.

My love the dun fellow
  who would sit at no board,
who would not seek to purchase
  a pint of ale or of beer;
a good double-distilled whisky
  you would not deign to drink –
you preferred the cress of the fountain
  and the restless water of the burn.

My love the noble lady
  in whom fault was never found,
who desired no cushion
  but the shoulder of the hill,
who suffered not the lead-shot
  to spark against her side:
Och, by the Virgin, it's my downfall
  I have not found you tonight!

Woman of the most mettlesome partner
  when rising with the dew:
in him you'd find no blemish
  and he would see only you;
you'd lie embracing each other
  on the very face of the peaks,
and then when the sun rose
  clear the light in your eyes.

When it came round to autumn
  I loved the rattle of your chest,
about to let out a bellow
  on the flat springy moor,
going to meet your sweetheart
  of the whitest tail and rump;
of the hinds she is the prettiest,
  of liveliest, most limber step.

XXXVIII. Rìgh na Cruinne ta gun Chrìch

Donnchadh nam Pìos

Donnchadh nam Pìos (c.1640–c.1700), Duncan MacRae of Inverinate in Kintail, was the compiler and scribe of the Fernaig manuscript, which he wrote over the period 1688–1693, contributing at least twelve of his own poems. He was strongly Epicopalian in religion and Jacobite in politics, and the manuscript reflects these interests. His wife was Seònaid, sister of Iain Garbh, MacLeod of Raasay (d.1671), the subject of no. XXXII.

Rìgh na cruinne ta gun chrìch,
　　Dèan mi cuimhneach ort gach tràth;
Na leig air sheachran mi
　　Air slighe ta baoith bàth.

Seòl mise san t-slighe cheart,
　　Rìgh nam feart ta fos ar cionn;
An leth aon-Iosa, do Mhac,
　　Math gach peacadh rinneadh liom.

Math dhom gach peacadh gu lèir
　　Do rinneadh liom fèin a ghnàth,
Agus saor-sa mi bho lochd
　　Bho is fiosrach thu nochd mar tàim.

Tàim-se nochd gu truagh,
　　Tàim-se truaillidh amo chorp;
Ta mo chridhe-sa fo leòn,
　　Ta peacadh bàis air mo lot.

Ach Fhir dh'fhuiling bàs ri crann
　　Le pianta teann is cam bhreith,
Dìon-sa mise, a Mhic mo Dhè,
　　Cuir-sa gu treun as mo leth.

Cruthaich unnam-s' cridhe nuadh,
　　Fhir a chaidh san uaigh gun lochd,
Bho is fiosrach thu mar a tà
　　An cridhe cnàmh namo chorp.

XXXVIII. King of the World without End

King of the world without end,
   make me mindful of you always;
do not suffer me to go astray
   on a path that is wicked and vain.

Guide me in the path that is right,
   King of all virtues in Heaven above;
forgive every sin committed by me,
   for the sake of Jesus, Your only Son.

Forgive utterly my every sin
   that I through habit have incurred,
and as You know how I am tonight
   deliver me from harm.

Tonight I am in deep despair,
   in my body I am corrupt;
my heart is wounded sore,
   mortal sin has me undone.

But Man who suffered death on the Cross
   with false judgement and agonising pains,
protect me, O Son of my God,
   do fierce battle for my sake.

Create in me a new heart,
   Man who went without sin to the grave,
since you know how the heart
   lies rotting in my frame.

Deònaich dhom aithrigh gu tràth –
Na leig-se mu làr mo dhìth,
Bho is tusa tobar gach gràis
Bhuaineadh as gach càs mi, a Rìgh.

Rìgh na cruinne etc.

XXXIX. Coille Chragaidh

Iain mac Ailein mhic Iain mhic Eòghainn

We have a considerable body of the verse of Iain mac Ailein (c.1655–1741), a Maclean poet: some of it is similar to 'village' poetry, better known from later times and often concerned with personalities and events primarily of local interest. Here, however, he is concerned with the great Jacobite victory at Killiecrankie on 27 July 1689, where Dundee routed the Williamite army under General Hugh Mackay of Scourie by means of the 'Highland charge'. The poet here gives special attention to the 300 Mull-men (possibly the poet was one of them) who were led there by the 19-year-old Sir Iain of Duart, and to the Irish contingent of 300 men. But despite the title the song seems really to have been inspired by the 'Act' mentioned in stanza 5, which is probably the 'Proclamation of Indemnity' issued by the Privy Council on behalf of king William on 27 August 1691: this offered pardon to Jacobites who had fought at Killiecrankie, on condition that they 'render themselves in subjectione to our authority and laues, humbly asking pardone for what is past'.

'N àm dhol sìos, 'n àm dhol sìos,
'N àm dhol sìos bu deònach
Luchd nam breacan, luchd nam breacan
A leigeadh le mòintich
A' folbh gu dian, a' folbh gu dian
Gun stad re prìs, an òrdugh,
An dèidh a' ghunna an claidheamh ullamh
Gun dad tuilleadh *motion*.

Do not abandon me in my need,
    grant me penitence in time;
for You are the well of each grace
    that could pluck me from all danger, King.

XXXIX. Killiecrankie

When charging down, when charging down,
when charging down, undaunted,
the men in plaid, the men in plaid
who would rush down the hillside,
pressing on keenly, pressing on keenly,
stopping for nothing, in order,
after the gun the sword ready
without any more motion.

Mhaighstir Cailein, tha mi deimhinn
Gun d'fhuair thu barrachd fòghlaim:
Is fior gun bheum do neach fon ghrèin
A dh'fhàg do bheul an t-òran.
Cha b'fheàrr do bheus na tràill no bèist
Mur b'oil leat Seumas fhògar,
'S a thricead dh'òrdaich e gun dearmad
Airgead agus òr dhuit.

'S iomadh neach dh'a robh e ceart
Nach d'rinn a' bheart bu chòir dhaibh:
Re àm a fheuma, Sasann thrèig e,
Alba is Eirinn còmhla;
Armailt rìoghail làidir lìonmhor
'Ga robh na cìsean mòra,
Cho luath 's a chunnairc iad Rìgh Uilleam
Cha d'rinn iad tuilleadh còmhraig.

Cha b'e ghealtachd thug dhaibh snasadh
'S cha b'e neart Phrionns *Orange*,
Ach dearmad dìreach thighinn nan inntinn
On do chinn iad deònach
M'an rìgh dùthcha fèin a dhiùchar
Air son diùc na Fòlaint:
Ach facal soitheamh duirt neach roimhe
Gum bi gach nodha rò gheal.

Ma thèid an Achd-sa an leud no am fad
Chan fheàrr gach neach na òglach:
Còir aig lag, cha diong i dad
Mur faigh e neart dh'an connsachadh.
Am mac a' gabhail brath air athair
Leis a' chlaidheamh chòmhraig,
Chualas riamh gum b'ann don ghnìomh sin
Nach robh Dia ga òrdachadh.

Master Cailean, I am sure
that you should know better:
it is clear without doubt to anyone on earth
that you gave up the singing.
No better your ways than a slave or beast's
if you were not galled by James' exile,
considering how often and without fail
he consigned you gold and silver.

Many people to whom he had been just
did not do the deed they ought to:
in the time of his need England forsook him,
Scotland and Ireland together;
a numerous strong royal army,
raised by high taxation,
as soon as they saw king William
they would do no more battle.

It was no cowardice that gave them order
nor the strength of the Prince of Orange,
but simply oblivion entering their heads
from which they soon grew fervent
to banish the king of their own country
in favour of the Duke of Holland:
but a wise saying long since uttered
tells that anything new seems brighter.

If this Act is enforced far and wide
each man will be no better than a youngster:
justice for the weak, it can effect not a thing,
unless he gets the strength to argue.
The son taking advantage of his father
with the sword of combat,
it was never heard it was for that deed
that God ever ordained him.

Ga b'e aca, nighean no mac,
A leugh gum bu cheart an seòl doibh
Crùn an athar fèin sa' chathair
A ghabhail le fòirneart,
Is sgainnil bhrèige a chur an cèill
A chaoidh nach feudte chòmhdach:
Tha Tì dh'an lèir, mas i so an eucoir –
Soirbh dho fèin a tòrachd.

Dham bharail fèin, ga beag mo lèirsinn,
Gheibh mi ceud ga chòmhdach,
Ge b'e tì dhe'n dèan Dia rìgh
Gur còir bhith strìocadh dhò-san;
'S gad thomhais e ceum d'a làn-toil fèin
'S gun e cur èiginn òirne,
Saoil sibh pèin an lagh no reusan
Dol a leum na sgròban?

Sgeula uam-sa mu Raon Ruaidhri
An robh na sluaigh a' còmhrag:
Chuid as luaithe ghabh an ruaig dhiubh
Bu daoine uaisle còir iad!
Nan cumte suas riu teine is luaidhe,
Ris an d'fhuair iad fòghlam,
'S tearc a chruinnich riamh an uiread
Gheibheadh urram beò dhiubh.

Ach luchd a' chunnairt chleachd na buillean
'S nach d'fhuair tuilleadh fòghlaim,
Nach do leugh an Achd mar dhìon d'am pearsain –
Gum b'e an staid bu chòir dhoibh
Ach gach tì nach tuit bhith shìos nan uchd
An còmhraig uilc bu nòs doibh:
Man do phill na gillean 's iomadh pinne
Thug sgeana biorach Thòmais.

Whichever of them, son or daughter,
that read it would be their right action
to take away the crown by force
from their own enthroned father,
and to put about scandalous lies
that never could be proven:
the One who sees all, if this is a wrong –
it is easy for Him to pursue it.

I am of the opinion, though limited my vision,
I will get a hundred to confirm it,
that whoever the man God makes king
to submit to him is proper;
and though he behaved just as he pleased
but without putting us to trouble,
do you think by law or reason
of leaping up at his gullet?

News I have about Killiecrankie
where the hosts were fighting;
those of them who were soonest routed
they were well-to-do nobles!
If they had been provided with fire and lead,
in which they had got training,
rarely would there gather so many alive
who could have received such honour.

But the dangerous men who just struck blows
and had no other training,
read not the Act as a shield for themselves –
for them the best way of proceeding
was to be down on top of those who fell not
in bitter conflict as was their custom:
before the lads returned it is many a stab
that Tòmas' sharp dirk inflicted.

Air each glè-mhòr cruidheach ceumnach
Sleamhainn steudmhor mòdhar,
Cha bu lapach an aois macaibh
Ceanntard feachd na Dreòllainn
Le bhuidheann threunfhear nach tais èirigh,
Ga robh croidhe treun mar leòghann:
'S iad a dh'èigh an ciad *retreat*
An dèidh luchd Beurla is cleòca.

Bha re sgèith sin buidheann èiginn
Dh'fholbh à Eirinn còmhla,
Re mionaid èabhla phàigh an èirig
Fèin le gleus an còmhraig;
Bu bhinn an sgeul bhith seal gan èisdeachd
'S iad ri èigheachd crònain,
'S a liuthad fear air bheagan ceannaich
A fhuair malaird còta.

Cha bu ghealtach bhith gan seachnadh –
Cha robh am faicinn bòidheach:
An lèintean paisgte fui'n dà achlais
'S an casan gun bhrògan;
Boineid dhaite a' dìon an claiginn
'S an gruag na pasgan fòithe,
Bu chosamhla an gleus ri treudan bhèistean
Na ri luchd cèille còire.

XL. Oran Murtadh Ghlinn Comhann

On 13 February 1692, soldiers billeted on the MacDonalds of Glencoe set out to kill them on an order signed by king William; about 38 people died. In the source used here (but no other) this poem is ascribed to 'Am bàrd Mucanach' ('the Muck poet'), who is otherwise unknown: it has been suggested that this name is an error for 'Am bàrd Mathanach' ('the Matheson poet'), and that the poet was in fact Murchadh MacMhathain (c.1670–c.1757), a well-known poet associated with the Earls of Seaforth. There is a tradition that Murchadh was in Glencoe on the night of the massacre.

On a great horse, shod and high-stepping,
sleek, composed and stately,
not feeble for his boyish years
the chief of the host of Mullmen,
with his troops of strongmen not slow in rising,
his heart like a lion was mighty:
it is they who yelled the first retreat
after the men of English and cassocks.

At that wing a terrible host
who left from Ireland together,
with a minute of fire they paid for themselves,
with the method of their combat;
sweet the tidings to hear them a while
as with the charge they bellowed,
with so many men of scanty means
who got a coat for their trouble.

There was nothing cowardly about avoiding them –
the sight of them was not lovely;
their shirt-tails caught up under their oxters
and their feet without footwear;
garish bonnets to protect their skulls
with their hair matted below them,
their get-up was more like herds of beasts
than men of justice and reason.

XL. A Song on the Massacre of Glencoe

Mìle marbhaisg air an t-saoghal!
    Tha e carach mar chaochladh nan sìon,
Nì nach guidheamaid fhaotainn,
    Mar na sruthaibh ag aomadh a-nìos;
'S i chneadh fèin thar gach adhbhar
    Bhios gach duine ga chaoineadh 's e tinn:
Breith Mhic Samhain air saoidhean
Teachd a ghleac rinn a thaobh cùl ar cinn.

A Rìgh fheartaich na grèine
    Tha an cathair na fèileadh, dèan sìth
Ri clann an fhir a bha ceutach,
    Nach bu choltach ri fèileadh fir chrìon;
Nuair thogta leat bratach,
    Crainn caola, fraoch daite agus pìob,
Bhiodh mnà gaoil le fuaim bhas
    A' caoidh laoch nan arm sgaiteach san strì.

Gun robh aigne duine uasail
    Aig a' bhaile agus uaidh ann ad chòir;
Cha bu ghèire gun tuigse
    Bha fui bheul bu neo-thuiteamach glòr;
Ceann na cèille is na cuideachd,
    Rinn na h-eucoraich cuspair de t'fheòil:
Cha b'e am breugair a mhurtadh
    Aig luchd shèideadh nam pluicean air stòl;

Ach duine mòr bu mhath cumadh –
    Bu neo-sgàthach an curaidh gun ghìomh:
Cha robh bàrr aig mac duine ort
    Ann an àilleachd 's an uirigleadh cinn;
Anns a' bhlàr bu mhaith t'fhuireach,
    Cosnadh làrach is urram an rìgh:
Mo sgread chràiteach am fulachd
    Bha as-taigh chlàraidh 'm biodh furan nam pìos!

On the world a thousand curses!
  like the fickle elements its deceit,
we get a thing we would not ask for,
  like the rivers tumbling down;
it is his own wound beyond everything
  each man will lament when he is hurt:
Mac Samhain's ensnaring of heroes
  was a trapping of us behind our backs.

O miraculous King of the sunshine
  on the throne of promise, make peace
with the children of the man who was handsome,
  whose generosity a niggard could not match;
when you raised a banner,
  slender shafts, coloured heather and pipes,
loving women with beating hands
  mourned the heroes armed fiercely for strife.

The spirit of a nobleman
  was near you at home and away;
no acuteness devoid of understanding
  came from the mouth of unfaltering voice;
head of reason and convivial people,
  the unjust made a target of your flesh:
it was not the liar who was murdered
  by those who blew out their cheeks on a stool;

But a big man of fine figure –
  fearless was the hero without fault:
no man could surpass you
  in handsomeness or eloquence of speech;
in the battle good your persistence,
  defending the position and honour of the king:
my sore cry the blood-bath
  in the panelled house of welcoming cups!

B'iad mo ghràdh na cuirp gheala
  Bha gu fiùghantach fearail neo-chrìon:
'S mairg a chunnairc ar n-uaislean
  Dol fo bhinn an luchd fuatha gun dìon;
Ach nam biomaid nar n-armaibh
  Mun do chruinnich an t-sealg air an tìr,
Gun robh còtaichean dearga
  Gun dol tuilleadh a dh'armailt an rìgh.

Cha b'e cruadal an cridhe
  Thug dhoibh buainteachd air buidhinn mo rùin:
Tilgeadh luaidhe na cithibh,
  Sud a' chùis a bha mishealbhach dhùinn;
Eadar uaislean is mhithibh
  Gun robh bhuaidh ud a' rith oirnn bho thùs:
Bu linn toiseach na slighe,
  Bhiodh na sluaisdean a' frithealadh dhùinn.

Cha b'i sud an fhuil shalach
  Bha ga taomadh mun talamh sa' ghleann,
'S a liuthad ùmaidh mar ghearan
  Bha cur fùdair na dheannaibh mu'r ceann.
A Rìgh dhùilich nan aingeal,
  Gabh-sa cùram d'ur n-anam 's sibh thall:
Chaidh ur cunntas an tanad
  Le garbh dhùsgadh na malairt a bha ann.

Thrus do chinneadh ri chèile
  Dhèanamh coinnimh an-dè anns an dùn;
Cha d'aithris thu sgeula,
  Fhir a b'urradh a rèiteach gach cùis;
Eiteag dhaingeann an sgèith thu
  Is am baranta treun air an cùl:
'Bidh là eile ga rèiteach,
  'S mise druidte fo dhèilibh san ùir.'

I loved the white corpses
   that had been generous, manly and brave:
woe to the one who saw our nobles
   condemned by their enemies without a chance;
but if we had been ready for combat
   before the hunt gathered force in the land,
impossible for the red-coats
   to return to the ranks of the King.

It was not bravery of heart
   that let them reap down the people I loved:
but firing lead-shot in showers,
   an unfortunate aspect for us;
both commoners and nobles,
   we were bound to be overcome from the start:
we were setting out on the journey,
   shovels preparing our grave.

That blood was not tainted
   that was spilled on the ground in the glen,
with so many complaining cowards
   sending gun-powder rushing past our heads.
O Creator King of the angels,
   take care of your souls on the other side:
your number has been diminished
   by the rough awakening of what took place.

Your kinfolk gathered together
   for a meeting yesterday in the fort;
you made no contribution,
   O man who could bring peace to any affair;
you are the strong feather of their wing
   and the firm warrant behind them:
'There'll be another day for arbitration
   when I'm locked under deal-boards in earth.'

Gu bheil mise fo mhulad
   Bhith 'g amharc ur gunna air stèill –
Sàr ghiomanach ullamh
   Leis an cinneadh an fhuil anns a' bheinn;
Ann am frìth nan damh mullaich,
   Far an dèantar libh munasg air seilg,
Ga bu tric sibh gan rùsgadh
   Cha d'iarr sibh riamh cunntas sna bèin.

Cha bu sgàthairean gealtach,
   Bhiodh a' maoidheadh an gaisgidh gach là,
Tha san eilean nan cadal
   'S nach dùisg gus an faicear am bràth;
Luchd dhìreadh nan Eitbheann
   Le cuilbheirean gleusda air an làimh;
'S lìonmhor fear nach d' rinn èirigh
   Bha na ghiomanach treun air a h-eàrr.

Cha d'fhuair sibh riamh lèigh
   A leigheas nan creuchd gu bhith slàn;
A' call na fala fo an lèintibh
   Bha na fir bu mhòr fèile ri dàimh;
Nam b'e Cothrom na Fèinne
   A bhiodh eadar sibh fèin 's Clanna Gall
Bhiodh eòin mholach an t-slèibhe
   A' gairsinn salach air creubhagan càich.

'S lìonmhor fear tha toirt sgannail
   Don tighearna òg tha air an fhearann so thall
Eadar Ceann Locha Raineach
   'S Rubha Shlèite is Bun Gharaidh nam beann:
Bha thu at fhèicheamh glè dhaingeann
   Far an èisdeadh ri d' theanga an cainnt,
Mar urball peucaig ga tharraing
   'S mar ghath reubaidh na nathrach gu call.

I am filled with sorrow
    seeing your gun on a stand –
excellent adroit huntsman
    who caused the blood to flow on the hill;
in the topmost stags' forest,
    of the quarry you would make chaff,
though you skinned them often
    you never demanded a share of the hides.

They were no faint-hearted cowards,
    boasting of their bravery each day,
that are sleeping on the island
    and will not waken now till Doom;
men who would climb the hills of Etive
    with highly-tuned guns in their arms;
many the one who has not risen
    was a fine marksman taking aim.

You never found a physician
    who can heal all wounds to the last;
the men generous to poets
    were losing blood beneath their shirts;
if there had been fair play
    between yourselves and the Lowland clans
the shaggy birds of the hillside
    would be squawking over others' dead.

Many the man spreading scandal
    of the young chief of the land over there
lying between Kinloch Rannoch,
    the point of Sleat and Bun Gharaidh of the hills:
you were a creditor most steadfast
    where your tongue was heeded in speech,
like the spread tail of a peacock,
    for destruction like the searing bite of the snake.

Leum an stiùir far a claiginn
  Le muir sùigh 's gun sinn achainteach dhò,
Dh'fhalbh na croinn 's na buill bheairte
  Is leig sinn ualach na slaite air an sgòd.
'S bochd an dùsgadh sa' mhadainn
  So fhuair sinn gu grad a teachd oirnn:
Ma gheibh sinn ùine ri fhaicinn
  Bheir sinn fùcadh mu seach air a' chlò.

XLI. Oran do Mhac Leòid Dhùn Bheagain

An Clàrsair Dall

Ruaidhri MacMhuirich (Morrison, c.1656–c.1714), the Blind Harper, a native of Lewis, was brought to Skye by Iain Breac, MacLeod of Dunvegan, probably in 1681, and given land at An Claigeann, near Dunvegan, where he was a tacksman. Iain Breac died in 1693 and his son and successor, Ruaidhri (d.1699), the subject of this song, had little regard for the traditions of his family, spending large amounts of his clan's rents extravagantly in Edinburgh. Among those criticised in the song is Uilleam Màrtainn, the chief's personal servant.

Miad a' mhulaid tha am thadhal
Dh'fhàg treaghaid am chliabh co goirt,
  On a rinneas air m'adhart
Ad dheaghaidh an triall gun toirt;
  Tha mis ort an tòir,
Is mi mios gu robh còir agam ort,
  A mhic athar mo ghràidh,
Is tu m'aighear, 's tu m'àdh, 's tu m'olc.

Chaidh a' chuibhle mun cuairt,
Ghrad thionndaidh gu fuachd am blàths:
  Gum faca mi uair
Dùn ratha nan cuach 'n seo thràigh,
  Far 'm biodh tathaich nan duan,
Iomadh mathas gun chruas, gun chàs:
  Dh'fhalbh an latha sin uainn,
'S tha na taighean gu fuarraidh fàs.

The rudder has lept from its socket
   in a high sea but not at our request,
the masts have gone and the halyards
   and the boom we let fall against the sail.
Wretched the waking in the morning
   we suddenly found to have dawned:
if we are granted the time to see it
   we will take our turn at waulking the cloth.

XLI. A Song to MacLeod of Dunvegan

   I am haunted by great sorrow
that has left a piercing pain in my chest,
   since I set out behind you
on a journey to no avail;
   I am hunting you down
as I judge that on you I had some claim,
   O son of the father I loved,
you are my joy, and my fortune, and my hurt.

   The wheel has gone round,
the warmth has abruptly turned cold:
   but here I have seen
a fort flourishing with cups now dry,
   a fort filled with songs,
bountiful without caution or stint:
   but that day has passed,
and the buildings are deserted and cold.

Chaidh Mac-alla as an Dùn
An am sgarachdainn dùinn ri 'r triath;
'S ann a thachair e rium
Air seacharan bheann is shliabh;
Labhair esan air thùs:
'Rèir mo bheachd-sa gur tu, mas fior,
An seo chunnaigheas air mhuirn
Roimh 'n uiridh an Dùn nan cliar.'

A Mhic-alla nan tùr,
'S e mo bharail gur tu 'n seo bhà
Ann an talla nam fiann
Ri aithris air gnìomh mo làmh.
'Ta mi 'm barail gur mi,
'S gum bu deacair dhomh fhìn bhith 'm thàmh,
'G èisdeachd broslaim gach ceòil
Ann am fochar Mhic Leòid an àidh.

'An am èirigh gu moch
Ann an tèaghlach gun sproc, gun ghruaim,
Chluinnte glèadhraich nan dos,
Is an cèile air a cois on t-suain;
An tràth ghabhadh i làn,
Is i chuireadh os àird na fhuair
Le meòir chionalta ghnìomhach
Dhrithleannach dhìonach luath.

'Bhiodh an rianadair fèin
Cur a dh'fhiachaibh gur h-e bhiodh ann,
E 'g èirigh nam miosg,
'S an èighe gu tric na cheann;
Cha bu truagh leinn an glaodh
'N uair a thuairgneadh se ì gu teann,
Cur a thagradh an cruas
Le h-aideachadh luath is mall.

Echo deserted the Dùn
at the time we were parted from our chief;
   I met with him
wandering hill and moor;
   it was he who spoke first:
'If I'm not mistaken, it was you
   I saw entertained
over a year ago in the Dùn of poet-bands.'

   O Echo of the forts,
I believe it was you who were there
   in the Fenians' hall,
copying the work of my hands.
   'I believe it was I,
and hard it would have been to keep quiet
   listening to the music's stir
in the presence of MacLeod of grace.

   'When it was time to rise
there was heard in that house without gloom
   the skirl of the drones
with their spouse afoot after sleep;
   when she had taken her fill,
she gave out all she had got,
   with agile fingers, kind,
sparkling, nimble and fleet.

   'The player himself
asserting that he was there,
   rising in their midst,
their calls resounding in his head;
   we pitied not their cries
when he tightly crushed the bag,
   setting out his theme
with a response quick then slow.

'An tràth chuirte na tàmh i
Le furtachd na fàrdaich fèin,
Dhomh-sa b'fhurasd a ràdh
Gum bu chuireideach gàir nan teud,
    Le h-iomairt dhà làmh
Cur am binnis do chàch an cèill:
    Rìgh, bu shiùbhlach ri m' chluais
An lùthadh le luasgan mheur.

'Anns an fheasgar na dhèidh,
An am teasdadh don ghrèin tràth-nòn',
Fir ag cnapraich mun chlàr
Is cath air a ghnàth chur leò;
    Dà chomhairleach gheàrr
Gun labhairt, ge b'àrd an glòir,
    'S a Rìgh, bu tìtheach an guin
Do dhaoine gun fhuil, gun fheòil.

'Gheibhte fleasgaich gun ghràin
Cur ri macnas gun sgràth, gun fhuath,
    Is mnài fhionna 'n fhuilt rèidh
Cur an grinnis an cèill le stuaim;
    An dèidh ceilearadh beòil
Dannsa oileanach òrdail suas,
    Le fear bogha nan còir
Chumail modha ri pòr an cluas.

'Bho linn nan linntean a bhà mi
Mar aonduine tàmh sa' chùirt,
    'S theireadh iomadh Mac Leòid
Mach b'uireasbhaidh eòlais dùinn;
    Ach na fhasadh gun fheum
Chan fhaca mi fèin bho thùs
    Ri fad mo chuimhne-sa riamh
Gun taighteir, gun triath an Dùn.'

'When she was laid to rest
relieved in her own place,
    I could say with ease
how frisky the cry of the strings,
    under the play of two hands
drawing out their sweetness for all:
    God, rippling in my ears
their variation by fingers swift.

    'In the evening after that
when the afternoon sun would expire,
    men shaking dice at the board,
waging battle as was their wont;
    two counsellors squat
without speech, though rattling loud,
    and how venomous their spite
towards men without flesh, without blood.

    'Young men whom none disdained
courting without impropriety or cheek,
    and fair women of smooth hair
modestly revealing their charms;
    after the singing of songs,
there'd be dancing, well-tutored, exact,
    nearby a musician with his bow
keeping the measure in their ears.

    'From the earliest generation
I lived like another at court,
    and many a MacLeod would say
he suffered not for his acquaintance with me;
    but from the beginning I never saw
the Dùn as a useless shell,
    nor as far as I recollect
was it ever without tutor or lord.'

Ach on ràinig thu aois,
Tha ri ràitinn gur baoth do ghlòir:
    Chan e fasadh a th' ann,
Ged a tha e san am gun lòd;
    Air taighteir 's beag fheum
Is òg-thighearna fèin na lorg,
    'S e ri fhaotainn gun fheall
Cur ri baoith ann an ceann luchd chleòc.

Cha bhi 'm pèidse ann am meas
Mur bi eudach am fasan chàich;
    Ged chosd e ginidh an t-slat –
Gheibhear siod air son mart sa' mhàl;
    Urad eile ri chois,
Gun tèid siod ann an casag dhà,
    'S briogais bheilibheid mhìn
Gu bhith gabhail mu ghaoith a mhàis.

Cha bhi 'm pèidse ann am prìs
E gun snàithe dh'a dhìth ach cleòc;
    Giort a' chlaidheimh cha b'fhiach,
'S bu chùis athais ceann iarainn dò:
    Crios dealbhach on bhùth,
Bogh' chinn airgid is biùgail òir –
    'S fheudar faighinn sin dà:
'S thig air m'fhearann-sa màl nas mò.

Thèid Uilleam Màrtainn a mach
Glè stràiceil air each 's e triall –
    Is co àrd e na bheachd
Ris an àrmann a chleachd bhith fial;
    Cha ghlacar leis crann,
Cas-chaibe na làimh cha b'fhiach,
    'S e cho spaideil ri diùc,
Ged bha athair ri bùrach riamh.

But since you've grown old,
it is said your voice is without use:
   the building is no shell
though it lacks now its usual folk;
   of a tutor it has small need
with its own young chief in his place,
   shamelessly going to waste
in the company of Lowland fops.

The page commands no respect
unless his attire accords with the rest;
   though it cost a guinea the yard –
it is got for a mart paid as rent;
   the same again
will go on a doublet for him,
   with fine velvet trews
to wrap up the wind round his bum.

Not costly enough the page
if he lacks as little as a cloak;
   a sword-girth would be no good,
its iron hilt a cause for shame:
   but a shop-fashioned belt,
a golden bugle and silver-tipped bow –
   those he must get:
and the rent on my land will go up.

Uilleam Martainn sets out
bombastic, riding on his horse –
   in his own regard as high
as that chief who made generosity his way;
   a plough he will not touch,
below his dignity a spade in his hand,
   though he is as dapper as a duke,
his father always rooted about in the soil.

Thoir teachdaireachd uam
Le deatam gu Ruaidhri òg,
Agus innis da fèin
Cuid d'a chunnart giodh e Mac Leòid;
Biodh e 'g amharc na dhèidh
Air an Iain a dh'eug 's nach beò:
Gum bu shaidhbhir a chliù,
Is chan fhàgadh e 'n Dùn gun cheòl.

A Mhic-alla 'n seo bhà
Anns a' bhaile 'n robh gràdh nan cliar,
An triath tighearnail teann,
Is an cridhe gun fheall na chliabh –
Ghabh e tlachd dh'a thìr fèin,
'S cha do chleachd e Dùn-èideann riamh;
Dh'fhàg e 'm bannach gun bheàrn,
'S b'fheàrr gun aithriseadh càch a chiall.

XLII. Cumha Choire an Easa

Am Pìobaire Dall

Iain MacAidh (Mackay, 1656–1754), the Blind Piper, was born in Gairloch, Wester Ross, the son of Ruaidhri MacAidh, also a piper, who had come there from Sutherland. Iain was acquainted with An Clàrsair Dall. He probably composed this song in or after 1696, the year of the death of Colonel Robert Mackay (stanzas 1 and 4), son of the second Lord Reay. Coire an Easa is to the south of the path which runs east from Achfary, near Loch Stack in Sutherland, towards Gleann Gollaidh and the southern side of Ben Hope.

'S mi an-diugh a' fàgail na tìre,
Siubhal na frìthe air a lethtaobh,
'Se dh'fhàg gun airgead mo phòca
Ceann mo stòrais fo na leacaibh.

Take this message from me
to young Ruaidhri with all possible speed,
   and tell him though he is MacLeod
something of the danger he is in;
   let him look back
at the Iain who died and is no more:
   rich was his renown,
without music he never left the Dùn.

O Echo that was in the hall
where dwelt the love of poet-bands,
   the solemn stately chief
with the guileless heart in his breast –
   in his own land he took delight,
with Edinburgh he bothered not at all;
   he left the bannock without gap,
better if others copied his good sense.

XLII. A Lament for Coire an Easa

Slowly, with feeling.

Today as I leave the country,
   skirting the edge of the moorland,
what has left my pocket without money
   is my patron lying under the flagstones.

'S mi aig bràigh an Alltain Riabhaich,
  'G iarraidh gu Bealach na Fèitheadh,
Far am bi damh dearg na cròic
  Mu Fhèill an Ròid re dol san dàmhair.

'G iarraidh gu bealach an easa
  Far an tric a sgapadh fùdar,
Far am bi mìolchoin gan teirbhirt,
  Cur mac na h-èilde gu dhùlan.

Coire gun easbhaidh gun iomrall:
  'S tric bha Raibeart ma do chomraibh;
Gach aon uair a nì mi t'iomradh
  Tuitidh mo chridhe fo thromchradh.

"Se siod mise, Coire an Easa,
  Ta mi nam sheasamh mar b'àbhaist;
Ma ta tus nat fhear ma ealain
  Cluinneamaid annas do làimhe.'

'N àill leat mise rùsgadh ceòil dhuit,
  'S mi am aonar an ceò air bhealach
Gun spèis aig duine ta beò dhiom
  On chuaidh an còirneal san talamh?

Mo chreach 's mo thùirse is mo thruaighe
  San uair-se ga chur dhomh 'n ìre,
An comann chumadh rium uaisle
  San uaigh an-diugh gun an dìreadh.

Nan creideadh tu fèin so, a Choire,
  Gura dorran sud air m'inntinn,
Gur cuid de dh'adhbhar mo leisgeil
  Nach faod mi seasamh ri seinn dhuit.

'Beannachd dhuit agus buaidh làrach
  Anns gach àit an dèan thu seasamh
A chionn do phuirt bhlasda dhìonaich,
  'S a' ghrian a' cromadh re feasgar.

I am on the bank of Alltan Riabhach,
   wanting across to Bealach na Fèitheadh,
where the russet stag of the antlers
   around Rood-day makes for the rutting.

Wanting across to the waterfall gully
   where lead-shot was often scattered,
where greyhounds are incited,
   the son of the hind held by their baying.

A corrie without defect or blemish:
   often was Raibeart at your waters-meeting;
every time your name I utter
   my heart falls into sadness.

'That is me, Coire an Easa,
   I am here just as ever;
if art is your business
   let's hear the skill of your handwork.'

Do you want me to bring you forth music
   all by myself in the mists in a byway,
lacking the respect of any man living
   since the Colonel went to the graveyard?

My undoing, my woe and my sorrow
   the moment I heard it related,
that the person who maintained me
   is in the grave today without rising.

If you would believe this, Coire,
   that it has left my mind in anguish,
it is part of the cause of my plea that
   I cannot stand and play before you.

'A blessing to you and victory in battle
   everywhere you take your playing
for the sake of your tune, eloquent and hearty,
   while the sun goes down in the evening.

''Se sud ceòl as binne thruaighe
 Chualas bho linn Mhic Aoidh Dòmhnaill;
'S grathann a bhios e nam chluasan,
 Am fuaim bha aig tabhann do mheòiribh.'

Ta cuid de mhaithibh na h-Eireann
 Re tighinn gu d' rèidhlean le h-ealain:
Ma sheinn Ruaidhri Dall dhuibh Fàilte
 Bha Mac Aoidh 's a chàirdean mar ris.

'S grianach t'ursainn fèin, a Choire,
 Gun fhiadh re teàrnadh gu d' bhaile;
Liuthad neach dha'm b'fhiach do mholadh,
 Do chrìoch chorrach fhiadhaich bhainneach.

Do chìob, do bhorran, do mhileach,
 Do leas, a Choire, gur lèanach
Lùbach luibheach daite diamhair;
 Gur fasgach do chuile is gur feurach.

Gu nòineanach gucagach mealach
 Lònanach lusanach iomrach,
'S bòrcach do ghorm-luachar mheallaidh
 Gun fhuachd na fearthainn ach ciùbhrach.

Do dheud mar uile-dhreach a' chanaich,
 Cìrean do mhullaich cha chreathnaich,
Far am bi na fèidh gu torrach
 'G èirigh faramach ma t'fhireach.

Gormanach tolmanach àlainn
 Lachach lusach dosach cràighiach,
Fradharcach gadharach breitheach
 Ag iomain na h-eilid gu nàmhaid.

Siumragach sealbhagach duilleach
 Mìnlachach gormleudach gleannach,
Coire riabhach riasgach luideach
 Far 'm biadhte chuideachd gun cheannach.

That is the music of the sweetest sadness
   heard since the time of Mac Aoidh, Dòmhnall;
for a while yet in my ears it will linger,
   that swift playing from your fingers.'

Some of the noble artists of Ireland
   come to your greenswards with learning:
if Ruaidhri Dall has played you a Fàilte
   Mac Aoidh and his friends were with him also.

Sunny your own door-post, fair Coire,
   without deer descending to your homestead;
so many people who could justly praise you,
   your whereabouts peaked, desolate, milky.

With your deer-grass, moor-grass, sweet-grass,
   flourishing, O Corrie, is your garden,
full of herbs and colours, winding, secret;
   your meadowy patch is sheltered, verdant.

Daisy-spangled, flowery, honied,
   lush and undulating, boggy,
your tussocks of green-rush bursting,
   no rain or cold, just drizzle.

Your teeth like cotton-grass in appearance,
   the combs of your height do not tremble,
where the numerous fecund deerherds
   rise up noisily about your incline.

With knolls and lovely green hillocks,
   dense and bushy, with duck and sheldrake,
a good look-out, a place for trapping
   the hind hounded towards her enemy.

Leafy, with clover and sorrel,
   camomile, green slopes and gullies,
brindled, tousled, ragged corrie,
   its company fed without payment.

'N àm don ghrèin dhol air a h-uilinn
Gasda glèidhteach reubach fuileach
Branach stràcach riachach finleach
Sealgach marbhach targnach giullach.

San àm a bhith teannadh gu d' rèidhlean
Teinnteach cinnteach ciallach cèireach
Fìonach stòpach còrnach teudach
Ordail eòlach òlar ceutach.

Ach siod mo dhùrachd dhuit, a Choire,
O tha mo dhùil re dol thairis,
'S gun mi ach tuisleach sa' mhonadh
'S mithich dhomh triall thun a' bhealaich.

XLIII. Do Chlainn Ghill-Eain

air do na Caimbeulaich buaidh fhaotainn orra

Mairghread nighean Lachlainn

Mairghread nighean Lachlainn (c.1660–post 1751) was a Mull poet, either a MacDonald or a Maclean. She is traditionally remembered as a 'bean tuiream', a woman whose function was to weep and and sing laments at funerals, but her extant works show her to have been very much concerned with clan and politics. This may be her earliest extant song. Somhairle MacGill-eain suggests that we can date the song to the period 1692–1704, when Sir Iain (d.1716), Maclean of Duart and son of Sir Ailean, was in exile following the completion in 1691 of the Campbell conquest of Mull. But we cannot be sure what (potential?) event, referred to in line 1d, gave rise to the song.

> *Cha choma leam fhèin no co-dhiù sin,*
> *Aon mhac Sir Ailein nan lùireach,*
> *Cuilean leòghann nan long siùbhlach,*
> *Bhith cur lasair ri aitreabh Dhuibhneach.*

When the sun is sinking on her elbow,
   well-protected the place for bloody tearing,
corn-husks and fennel, thumping and flaying,
   hunting, killing, gillies boasting.

When it is time to make for your meadow
   there is sensible talk, fire and candles,
wine in stoups, cups and music,
   orderly, experienced, pleasant drinking.

But here's my farewell to you, O Coire,
   since I need to be crossing over,
as I am only stumbling through the heather,
   it is time for me to set off for the byway.

XLIII. To Clan MacLean

I am neither displeased nor indifferent
for the one son of Sir Ailean of hauberks
– the lion cub who sails the swift vessels –
to be firing a house full of Campbells.

Ach a Fhir ris an dèanam m'ùrnaigh
'S mi mar Oisean an dèis a rùsgaidh,
Tionndaidh an roth is cuir far cùl i
Is cuir an tìr so air òrdugh dhùinne.

Nuair thàinig sibh siar an toiseach
Bha sibh buadhail anns gach cogadh –
Lanna cruaidhe, bhuailte goirt iad:
Chuirte feum air lèighe g'ar lota.

An àm dol sìos don dream Dhuibhneach
Dol suas le buaidh bu dual dhùinne;
'S fada chluinnte gàbh ar muinntir,
Togail faoibh air taobh gach tulchain.

Ach cò e an neach a tha gun mhùtha,
Mar na nialaibh air an aonach?
Cinne làidir nan lann rùisgte
Bhith mar tha iad roimh na Duibhnich!

Gu bheil m'inntinn-se fo smalan
Is mo shùilean gu bhith galach
Gus am faic mi rìs an latha
'Sam bi dol suas air sìol mo thaighe.

But God to whom I make my prayer,
while I exist like the ravaged Oisean,
turn the wheel and put it backwards,
and place this land under our dominion.

At first when you came westwards
you conquered us in every battle –
hard blades bitterly brandished:
for our wounds leeches were needed.

When the crew of Campbells are defeated
our own ascendancy would seem destined;
far should be heard our people's fury,
raising spoil on every hillside.

Who is the person time does not alter,
like the shadows of clouds on the mountain?
The strong tribe of swords unsheathed
standing powerless before the Campbells!

My spirit is sore and dejected
and my eyes will keep on weeping
until once more I see the day when
the people of my house will triumph.

Notes

I. Iomair Thusa, Choinnich Cridhe

From *An Gaidheal*, V (1876), p.49. For other versions see C. Ó Baoill and D. MacAulay, *Scottish Gaelic vernacular verse to 1730: a checklist*, Aberdeen University Department of Celtic, 1988 [*Checklist*], no.395; Alexander Carmichael, *Carmina Gadelica*, vol. VI, Edinburgh: Scottish Academic Press, 1971, p.14.

The tune here given is taken from *Tocher*, no.35, p.305, where it is transcribed from a performance in 1980 by the Reverend William Matheson: he learned the song from an aunt, a native of Lewis. It is clear from *Tocher* that, if we treat the lines given with the music here as a stanza, the second such stanza will begin with the second line of the poem (*Gaol nam ban òg . . .*) and contain also the third (*Tha eagal mòr . . .*); the third stanza will open with the third line, and so on throughout the poem. This form of 'rolling' stanza is common in the waulking song type.

II. A Mhic Iain Mhic Sheumais

From K.C. Craig, *Orain luaidh Màiri nighean Alasdair*, Glasgow: Matheson, 1949, p.2. For other versions see *Checklist*, no.373; Frances Tolmie's collection in *Journal of the Folk-Song Society*, no.16 (1911), pp. 255–257; John L. Campbell, *Songs remembered in exile*, Aberdeen University Press, 1990, pp. 98–99.

st.10: the idea of the lover sucking the hero's blood is found elsewhere in Gaelic songs (see Derick S. Thomson, *The companion to Gaelic Scotland*, Oxford: Blackwell, 1983, pp.78b, 81b), in early Gaelic literature and probably in 18th-century Irish verse.

line 12a: Craig has *curaidh*.

st.15: a note added in National Library [NLS] MS 3783, p.11b, says: 'Eriska, where Donald then lived [?was divided] between Neil og MacNeill of Barra and Allan Macdonald of Clanranald – Mac Iain Mhuideartaich', though genealogical works do not seem to confirm this.

The tune is taken from *Tocher*, no.35, p.304, where it is transcribed from a performance in 1980 by William Matheson; he got the tune from Donnchadh Clachair, Duncan MacDonald (1883–1954), Peninerine, South Uist. In the notes in *Tocher* the tune is described as 'unusual'.

Other sources make it clear that this song is sung in 'rolling' stanzas: 'Two couplets are sung as a verse, the last couplet of one verse forming the first couplet of the next' (Tolmie p.256).

III. MacGriogair à Ruaro

From MacLagan [ML] MS 99, pp.8–10. For other versions see *Checklist*, no.402. The title here (from ML) can be justified from other versions, such as that in W.J. Watson, *Bàrdachd Ghàidhlig* [BG], Stirling: Learmonth, 1959, line 6285, which mention the placename Ruaro (in Glenlyon, Perthshire). The song is studied in detail in Alasdair Duncan's unpublished 1979 MLitt thesis, *Some MacGregor songs*, in Edinburgh University Library, pp.108–127. A dating in the first quarter of the seventeenth century seems reasonable.

st.13: MacMhuirich appears to have been the name of the MacGregors' standard-bearer.

The tune is simplified from no.88 in Patrick McDonald, *A collection of Highland vocal airs*, Edinburgh, 1784, p.13, where it appears among the 'Perthshire Airs'. Here we have raised the A in bar 8 by an octave, because the higher note at this point seemed to us more likely in a traditional sung performance. A Skye tune appears in the Tolmie collection, p.261, where it is clear that the performance is in 'rolling' couplets forming quatrains: couplets 1 and 2 are first sung to the tune, then couplets 2 and 3, then 3 and 4, and so on.

IV. Ailean Dubh à Lòchaidh

From *An Gaidheal*, vol. LVIII (1963), p.3, where text, tune and background story are printed, but without any information as to provenance. A version of the song noted in 1946 from Raasay/Skye, in TGSI XXXIX/XL, p.181, is fairly close to this one.

The tune is taken from *An Gaidheal* LVIII, p.3.

V. An Spaidearachd Bharrach

From J.L. Campbell and Francis Collinson, *Hebridean folksongs*, vol. II, Oxford: Clarendon, 1977 [HF], pp.124–126, where it is taken from a manuscript written in Oban in the 1890s; this in turn probably derived its text from Colin Campbell, piper, an old soldier who was a native of South Uist (*ibid.*, p.188). Other versions are discussed on pp.232–233 there.

The tune is taken from HF, p.322, where it is noted from the singing of Mrs Neil Campbell (1868–1970), South Uist, in 1957.

VI. Thugar Maighdeann a' Chùil Bhuidhe

From *The Celtic Review*, vol. VII (1911), p.138, to which it was contributed by Alexander Carmichael (1832–1912).

VII. Do Ruaidhri Mòr, Mac Leòid

From Alexander Cameron, *Reliquiae Celticae*, II (Inverness, 1894), pp.284–285, where the text is that of the *Red Book of Clanranald* (manuscript MCR 39 in the Royal Museum, Edinburgh), and was written there by Niall (mac Dhòmhnaill) MacMhuirich (c.1637–1726); and from *Reliquiae Celticae*, I (1892), pp.121–122, the text of NLS MS 72.1.48 (folio 3a), which is also a South Uist manuscript of the period 1660–1680. The spelling used here is according to the Classical Gaelic norm. From these two sources Professor Thomson edited the poem in TGSI XLIX (1977), p.12.

Here we have made one major emendation, substituting *sine* for the word *lionmhur* which occurs in both manuscripts in line 1d. The change is made on metrical grounds: the word *lionmhur* there is the only significant metrical fault in the entire, very professional, poem, which is in strict *rannaigheacht mhór* (the metre sometimes designated 7^1+7^1, *i.e.* each line having seven syllables and ending with a monosyllable). The word *sine* is suggested as an improvement because it provides a missing (and necessary) internal rhyme (with *hibhe*) and a missing (and necessary) alliteration with *sluagh*.

Sine is the superlative form of *sean*, which normally means 'old', and in that sense is not very likely in the context of praise of heroes. But *sean* is used in Classical Gaelic verse to praise weapons, and has a meaning something like 'in long use, proven'; used of warriors it can mean 'veteran, experienced'. And in modern songs it is used as a similar compliment, a good example being our no.IX (st.21a-b), where the hero is called 'An t-òg as sine, / As feàrr den chinneadh': there *sine* can hardly mean 'oldest'.

If *sine*, then, was in Niall Mòr's original, perhaps it was emended by the scribes of the two manuscripts principally because the word *sean* was not, in their view as in ours, unambiguously complimentary.

line 4a: Olbhu(i)r, the Norse *Olvir*, is the name of at least two people in the pedigree of the MacLeods.

line 5d: sé: in Classical verse there is usually a *dùnadh* ('closure'), which means that the poem ends with a word, a phrase, a line or sometimes merely a syllable which repeats the opening of the poem. Other instances in this collection are nos XI–XIV, XVII, XVIII, XXXI, XXXIII and XXXVIII. Often the manuscripts point up the existence of the *dùnadh* by adding the repeated word(s) again at the end of the poem, as has happened with nos XI–XIV, XVIII, XXXIII and XXXVIII.

VIII. Tàladh Dhòmhnaill Ghuirm

From Craig, *Orain luaidh* (1949), p.11, a South Uist version. For other versions see *Checklist*, no.404, and HF, pp.128–130, 238; Catherine Kerrigan, *An anthology of Scottish women poets*, Edinburgh University Press, 1991, pp.18–22. Frances Tolmie tells us in her collection (p.239) that the song 'was originally sung as an "iorram" (rowing song), but became eventually a waulking-song'.

line 21: the reference here is to the custom, apparently common in the seventeenth-century Highlands, whereby the loser at cards or backgammon was struck with 'a single soled shoe, well plated, wherwith his antagonist was to give him six stroaks ane end, upon his bare loof, and the doeing of that with strenth and airt, was thought gallantry' (*Scottish Gaelic Studies* [SGS] IX, p.84).

The tune is from HF, p.325, where it is noted from the singing of Mrs Neil Campbell, South Uist, in 1957.

IX. Saighdean Ghlinn Lìobhainn

From MacNicol [MN] MS A, pp.17–20. For other versions see *Checklist*, no.413: a version in MacLagan [ML] MS 2 is probably the source of that in Gillies' collection (1786), pp.83–85, from which, in turn, derives the version in Watson's *Bàrdachd Ghàidhlig* [BG], pp.239–241. It seems to us, however, that ML is likely to derive from MN, and that MacLagan made changes to the text.

The title given here appears over the song in ML, and over the version in Gillies' collection, but it is not a very apt title. The song is a straightforward praise of a hero, using many of the commonplace episodes discussed in MacInnes' 'Panegyric code in Gaelic Poetry' in TGSI L, pp.435–498, and the arrows merely form part of one of these episodes; no. XIX is a very similar song.

line 6c: Barbarrachd MN, *Bairbeireachd* ML. Watson (BG, p.347) suggests 'barbwork' for *barbaireachd.*

lines 11a: T'saoidh in MN, altered to *tSaoi* in ML, *saoi* in Gillies. The word could evidently be feminine, as it could also in earlier Gaelic and in Irish verse.

line 17c: bhearcadach, with the first -a- short, gives a faulty rhyme. ML has *Bhairceideach*, as has Gillies, whence BG reads *bàrcaideach*, 'flowing, running in torrents'.

line 18c: ML writes *Airg-bhraiteach*, and above it adds: (*a.bhraisteach?* (perhaps thinking of a compound with *airgead*, meaning something like 'wearing silver brooches'). In BG, p.344, Watson explains *airgbhraiteach* as meaning 'clad in finely wrought mantles', but no other instance of the word seems to be known.

line 21a: MN reads: *An tog s shinne,* ML *shèine* with the *-h-* stroked out. Gillies (p.85) has *sine,* which BG (line 6387) emends to *finne.* On the meaning see notes on no. VII above.

X. Cumha do Niall Og

From *Notes & Queries of the Society of West Highland and Island Historical Research* [N&Q], first series, no.XXVI (1985), pp.4–8, with the omission of one difficult stanza. The text there is edited from two manuscripts, that of John Maclean, the Tiree poet (1787–1848), who took his manuscript to Nova Scotia with him in 1819; and the other written by Dr Donald Smith (1756–1805) and now in the NLS.

Neither source gives much information about the song, and the background is investigated by Nicholas Maclean-Bristol in N&Q, no. XXVII (1985), pp. 3–12. A traditional account of the death of the subject's father may be found in *The Celtic Monthly, XVI* (1908), p. 118.

line 6a-b: Mac Gill-eathain, the current chief of Duart, was doubtless Eachann Og (c.1578-c.1632), 14th of Duart; he was son of Sir Lachlann Mòr, 13th, who was killed at the battle of Tràigh Ghruinneard in Islay in 1598, and who is named in line 7c. The heir of the Cùil, a Maclean property in Islay, was Gill-eathain, another son of Sir Lachlann Mòr.

lines 7a-b: Mac Uimilein (in both manuscripts) is an unusual form of *Mac Uibhilein* (often anglicised 'MacQuillan'), the leader of the family which held the Route in County Antrim before losing it to the MacDonalds in the sixteenth century. One of these MacDonalds, Raghnall Arannach, became the first Earl of Antrim in 1620.

line 13b: both manuscripts write *innish,* but we take the word to be for the placename *Innis Choinnich,* an island off Mull where many of the Macleans were buried.

XI. Air Bas mhic Mhic Coinnich

From the transcription of the Fernaig manuscript (Gen.85 in Glasgow University Library) in Calum Mac Phàrlain, *Lamh-sgrìobhainn Mhic Rath: Dorlach Laoidhean,* Dun-De: Mac Leòid, [1923], pp.138–140.

On the words added at the end of this poem, and the next three, see Notes on no. VII above.

XII. Rainn do rinneadh leis na shean aois

From Mac Phàrlain, *Lamh-sgrìobhainn,* pp.140–142.

XIII. Ceithir rainn do rinneadh leis an là a d'eug se

From Mac Phàrlain, *Lamh-sgrìobhainn*, p.138.

XIV. Air Leabaidh a Bhàis

From Mac Phàrlain, *Lamh-sgrìobhainn*, p. 136.
The metre is a loose form of *deibhidhe* (7^x+7^{x+1}, *i.e.* seven syllables per line, and in each couplet the last stressed word of the second line will have one syllable more than the last stressed word of the first line).

XV. Coisich, a Rùin

From John L. Campbell, *Songs remembered in exile* [SRE], Aberdeen University Press, 1990, pp.123–125, for which it was recorded in 1937 from Mrs David Patterson, Benacadie, Cape Breton island, Canada. For other versions see *Checklist*, no.416; SRE, pp.232–233.
The tune is that used by Mrs Patterson, SRE, p.123.

XVI. Iorram do Shir Lachann

From the manuscript collection of Dr Hector Maclean of Grulin in Mull, compiled in the period 1738–1768 and now in the Public Archives in Halifax, Nova Scotia (numbered MG15G/2/2), p.107; published from there in C. Ó Baoill, *Eachann Bacach and other Maclean poets*, SGTS, 1972, pp.6–8. Here two stanzas are omitted, one because it is incomplete in the manuscript, the other because we do not fully understand it.

XVII. Sona do Cheird, a Chalbhaigh

From James Carney and David Greene, *Celtic studies: essays in memory of Angus Matheson, 1912–1962*, London: Routledge & Kegan Paul, 1968, pp.52–54, where the poem was edited by Professor Greene from the manuscript A v 2 in the Royal Irish Academy, Dublin. That manuscript was written by the poet himself, Cathal MacMhuirich, whose life and work Ronald Black discusses in 'The genius of Cathal MacMhuirich' in TGSI L (1977), pp.327–366. Two stanzas, incomplete in Greene's edition, are here omitted.
The metre is *deibhidhe* (7^x+7^{x+1}) but, as Black demonstrates (pp.337–338), the poet deliberately breaks the rules of *dán díreach* in stanzas 4–8, in order to point up the incompetence of An Calbhach; for instance, the rhyme *leamh: déanamh* in stanza 5 is imperfect, and there is no alliteration in line 8a.

XVIII. A Sheónóid Méadaigh Meanma

From *Éigse* (Dublin), vol. XI (1964), pp. 7–10, where the poem was edited by Angus Matheson from the manuscript E i 3 in the Royal Irish Academy. That manuscript was written by Cathal MacMhuirich, at some point after 1649, and Ronald Black (TGSI L, pp. 334–335) is in no doubt that Cathal was the author of the poem. The metre is *deibhidhe* (7^x+7^{x+1}).

XIX. Oran do Dhòmhnall Gorm Og, Mac Dhòmhnaill

From the Eigg collection of 1776, pp. 170–171, from which it is published in Annie M. Mackenzie, *Orain Iain Luim* [OIL], SGTS, 1964, pp.14–18; here we have omitted one difficult stanza.

This song can be read in close conjunction with John MacInnes' 'The panegyric code in Gaelic poetry and its historical background' in TGSI L (1978), pp.435–498, for the reader can easily see in it the various episodes which were *de rigueur* for a song of praise at the time. These include the weapons/hunting episode (stt.3–9), the allies episode (stt.11–12), the sea-faring episode (stt.14–17) and the evening entertainment/hospitality episode (stt.18–22).

lines 12a-b: Mac Mhic Ailein is the hereditary title of the chief of Clanranald, and Mac Mhic Alasdair of the chief of Glengarry (just as the title Mac Dhòmhnaill belongs to MacDonald of Sleat, see *The Clan Donald*, III, p.168).

line 19c: tàileasg, a medieval borrowing from French or English *tables*, denotes a board-game similar to (back)gammon, in which, as st. 22 indicates, dice were used, money was wagered and the dominant feature of the board was the series of 'points' (Gaelic *ti*, singular).

The tune given here is taken from Keith Norman Macdonald's *Gesto collection of Highland music*, Leipzig: Brandstetter, 1895–1902, Appendix, p.43, where it is entitled 'Domhnail nan Dun' and accompanied by a version of the text, and a left-hand part for piano performance. The music given is enough for two stanzas, so that it is likely that each stanza, apart from the first, is to be performed twice, once to each of the two melodic sections.

This tune is a close variant of that given below for no.XXX.

XX. Oran air Latha Blàir Inbhir Lòchaidh

From Turner's collection of 1813, pp.49–52; it is edited from this and other sources in OIL, pp.20–24. For a detailed account of the battle see David Stevenson, *Alasdair MacColla and the Highland problem in the seventeenth century*, Edinburgh: Donald, 1980, pp.151–163.

line 5a: this stanza is addressed to Sir Mungo Campbell of Lawers. A tale about him, and his boastfulness with the sword, appears in *Transactions of the Gaelic Society of Glasgow* V (1958), pp.32–34.

line 11c: the Campbells' ancestry includes at least one individual whose name was *Duibhne* (see W.D.H. Sellar, 'The earliest Campbells – Norman, Briton or Gael?', *Scottish Studies*, vol.17, part 2, pp.109–125), from whom members of the clan are called *Duibhnich*. Probably due to misinterpretation of the lenited form *Dhuibhne* or *Dhuibhnich*, the latter word often appears as *Guibhnich*.

stanza 15: it was evidently the forces led by Iain Mùideartach (d.1670), 12th chief of Clanranald since his succession in 1618, who captured Colin Campbell of Barbreck at the battle (Stevenson, *Alasdair MacColla*, p.161).

line 16d: George Gordon (1592–1649), 2nd Marquis of Huntly, 'the Cock of the North', whose lands included Strathbogie in Aberdeenshire, was at one point given the king's commission to lead the army, instead of Montrose (see Stevenson, *Alasdair MacColla*, pp.114–115, 120), and it may be that the poet is here giving the credit to Alasdair mac Colla for ensuring that Huntly was in the end disappointed in this.

line 17c: A feather from the inner corner of the wing was regarded as worthless. The prized feathers were those from the extremity of the wing and from the tail.

line 19b: Sir Lachlann Maclean of Duart (d.1649) joined Montrose at Inverlochy with only about twelve of his men.

The tune given here is a drastically simplified transcription from the heroic performance by James C.M. Campbell (1897–1979), a native of Kintail, on the School of Scottish Studies LP disc 'James Campbell of Kintail: Gaelic songs' (*Scottish Tradition* series, no.8; London: Tangent Records, 1984; TNGM 140). Since the text is of basically syllabic structure, the coincidence of notes and textual stress varies from stanza to stanza. The chorus, sung before each stanza, is to the same tune as the verses. Another transcription of James Campbell's tune appears in John Purser, *Scotland's music*, Edinburgh: Mainstream, 1992, p.133, and Purser comments: 'The triumphant song, with two confident octave leaps – the second higher in pitch – and a variety of rhythmic units in its short space that gives it tremendous vigour, sends out a musical challenge as magnificent as the belling of a stag in autumn.'

XXI. Turas mo chreiche thug mi Chola

From NLS MS 50.2.20, folios 182a–183a, written by John Dewar (1802–1872), probably around 1860 and probably from an Argyllshire informant or informants. The text is here divided into sections according to the final rhyme of the lines: in the manuscript there is similar breaking into sections, but it does not appear to be systematic. On folio 182b the song ends with the refrain vocables following line 40, and then we have six quatrains of *Crodh Chailein* and (in the hand of J.F. Campbell of

Islay) a quatrain in English. Next on folio 183a we have, unheaded, the remaining twelve lines followed by a somewhat different line of vocables: this may represent a different performance (by a different performer) from that of the text on f.182. A quite independent version of the song was published by Alexander Maclean Sinclair in TGSI XXVI, p.238, and the text there confirms that the two texts in Dewar's manuscript belong to the same song.

lines 21–22: lines very similar to these occur in another song in Campbell, *Songs remembered in exile* [SRE], p.245, lines 14–15 (cf. *Checklist*, no.1). Mac Dhonnchaidh Ghlinne Faochain was a Campbell landowner in Lorne, Argyllshire. It has been said that his name was Donnchadh and that he was killed at Inverlochy, and he is mentioned in Diorbhail Nic a' Bhriuthainn's famous song (Turner's collection, p.188, line 2) on Alasdair mac Colla. The SRE song has much in common with our song, and also presents a Campbell reaction to Inverlochy.

Cille Bhaodain is the parish church of Ardchattan on Loch Etive, a short distance north of Gleann Faochain.

lines 31–32: these lines are strongly reminiscent of the motif of the woman tied (sometimes by her hair) to a rock in the sea, to be drowned by the incoming tide. This is a fairly common motif in Highland tradition, especially in relation to Macleans, and there seems to be an instance of it in the tradition given in the introductory note to no. XXIII.

lines 49–51: the places named here are the lands of the Achnambreac family, including their main seat, Carnassary castle near Lochgilphead. *Bràigh(e) Ghlinne* might consist merely of two common nouns, 'high part of valley', but perhaps also it denotes the place appearing on maps as 'Breglen' or 'Bragleen', the holding of a prominent Campbell family near Gleann Faochain (cf. SRE, p.247).

The lament on the death of Dùghall Og (c.1642) refers to his lands as 'Clàr Ghiorra' (Cameron, *Reliquiae Celticae*, II, p.322), and the placename survives on maps in 'Lochgair'.

XXII. An Cobhernandori

From MacLagan [ML] manuscript 190, which has the date October 20th 1756; this seems to be the only source. Half of a sixth stanza, which was quite certainly addressed to Alasdair mac Colla, is omitted here.

The song has been published and studied by Allan Macinnes in 'The first Scottish Tories?', *The Scottish Historical Review*, vol. LXVII (1988), pp.56–66.

stanza 2 (chorus), line g: Professor Macinnes identifies the prince here as the Prince of Wales, later Charles II.

lines 3a–d: cf. Isaiah ii.4, Micah iv.3.

XXIII. *Bithidh 'n Deoch-sa an Làimh mo Rùin*

From Carmichael-Watson manuscript 58A in Edinburgh University Library, p.96, no.239. The scribe was Fr Allan McDonald (1859–1905), parish priest of Daliburgh in South Uist. The manuscript, written in 1888/1889, is a collection of assorted traditional lore from the southern Hebrides. This text gives only one line of refrain, and we have inserted the second line from the sung performance in *Tocher* 38 (see below).

This seems to have been a popular song: for other versions see *Checklist*, no.429; Campbell, *Songs remembered in exile*, p.157–161. In many sources it is accompanied by an explanatory tale, and some such tale is indeed necessary. We have prefaced to the text one which explains most points in our version (manuscript 58A has no explanatory tale).

It should be remembered that our version of the song is one of many, and that none of the extant versions reads like a fully coherent song text. Nor has any composite 'original' text been established.

stanza 7: it may be that this is a remnant of an instance of the 'emphatic antithesis' device discussed below in the Notes on no. XXIX. Perhaps a lost couplet, following this one, told how, far from having servants carrying meal to shops, the subject had men engaged in much more noble pursuits.

The tune used here is that published in *Tocher*, no.38 (1983), p.29, along with a text recorded in 1981 from Nan Eachainn Fhionnlaigh (Mackinnon, 1902–1982), Mingulay and Vatersay.

XXIV. *Oran do Thighearna Ghrannt*

From the Eigg collection [E](1776), pp.182–184, the only source we know of: the song does not appear to have been published elsewhere.

line 6f: E has *gum be t fhuaim*, which is probably faulty because it lacks a rhyme for *pudhar, dubha*, etc.

stanza 10: in Classical syllabic praise-poetry the poet would sometimes end by praising the subject's wife, and this practice is not uncommon in vernacular song too, as here and in no. XXVIII.

XXV. *Chailin òig as Stiùramaiche*

From Campbell and Collinson, *Hebridean folksongs*, vol. II (1977)[HF], pp.44–46, where it was recorded from the singing of Mrs Mary Morrison (Bean Phluim) in Barra in 1938. Other versions, and the history of the song, are discussed in detail in HF, pp.200–209.

The tune is that sung (solo) by Bean Phluim, HF, p.283. Each line of text is sung twice, once before each of the refrain lines.

XXVI. Oran Cumhaidh air Cor na Rìoghachd

From the Stewarts' collection (1804)[S], pp.416–418; also edited in OIL, pp.56–58.

line 4a: S has *foireigneadh*, which means 'oppression', 'tyranny'. But the rhyme-system suggests that the vowel between -*r*- and -*g*- must be an epenthetic vowel (as in *fearg*). Dwelly gives *fairgneadh* the meanings 'hacking' and 'sacking'; perhaps it is a form of the Classical Gaelic *argain* (genitive case *airgne*), from Early Gaelic *orgun*, 'slaying; ravaging'.

stanza 12: Niall MacLeod's father-in-law was John Munro of Lemlair.

lines 14c-d: as part of his reward for betraying Montrose, MacLeod of Assynt was given £20,000 Scots and 400 bolls of damaged meal from Leith (Mackenzie, *History of the Macleods*, pp.412–413).

XXVII. Do Mhac Leòid

From MacLagan [ML] MS 122, folio 4b–5a.
   An edition of this song in James C. Watson, *Gaelic songs of Mary Macleod*, London: Blackie, 1934, pp.20–24, is based on the Eigg collection (also in W.J. Watson, *Bàrdachd Ghàidhlig,* pp.181–183); there the subject is Sir Tormod of Berneray, and a tradition tells us that the poet composed it at his request, when he asked her what kind of a lament she would make for him when he died (pp. 113–114).
   This is perhaps the only song in ML for which a tune is also provided there. It follows directly on the text on folio 5a of MS 122, but we have no way of knowing whether or not it was MacLagan himself who wrote it (the text is in his hand). But though it includes such ornaments as trills, the music is not well written and is hard to interpret: there is neither key signature nor time signature. We have suggested these and emended various points in the music, so that the tune printed here is an arbitrary interpretation of that written in ML.
   There is music for two stanzas, and E (p.31) directs us to perform each stanza twice. It is therefore not unlikely that we are to sing this with the 'rolling' stanzas discussed above (for nos I–III), *i.e.* the music is fitted first to stanzas 1–2, then 2–3, 3–4 and so on.

XXVIII. Fuaim an Taibh

From the Eigg collection [E] of 1776, pp.27–31, which is the source of the version in the Stewarts' collection (1804), pp.219–224. Edited in J.C. Watson, *Gaelic songs of Mary Macleod*, pp.44–48; W.J. Watson, *Bàrdachd Ghàidhlig* (1959), pp.198–201.

line 2c: a reference, probably, to Pàdraig Mòr Mac Cruimein, who served the MacLeods as piper c.1640–1670; or possibly to his son Pàdraig Og, who served till after 1730.

line 8b: a reference to the Norse ancestry of the MacLeods, as in no. VII, line 4a.

line 23c: another allusion to the Norse origins of the MacLeods. On Mànas see William Matheson, 'The ancestry of the MacLeods' (1977), TGSI LI, pp. 71, 77.

The tune is taken from the Tolmie collection, p.262, no.98, where it was noted down from Margaret Gillies in Bracadale, Skye, in 1861. We have changed the music a little because it does not seem to have been well written. Tolmie may have forced it into too few bars, and the barring she gives does not fit the stress-pattern of the text.

There is music for only one stanza, though we are directed to repeat it. The directions with the text in E are not clear either: there we are told at stanza 1 to repeat the whole stanza, but at the remaining stanzas (from st.3 on) to repeat only the final line.

XXIX. Oran do Mhac Mhic Raghnaill na Ceapaich

From Turner's collection (1813), pp.101–103. Edited from this and other sources in Annie M. Mackenzie, *Orain Iain Luim* [OIL], pp.108–112.

stanzas 2–10: it is common in poetry to increase the impact of a complaint by prefixing to it mention of serious grievances (stt.2–5) and then saying they are nevertheless of minor importance, in comparison with the last one to be mentioned (st.6). James Ross calls this device 'emphatic antithesis' (*Éigse* VIII, p.13). Stanzas 8–10 look like another series (of sounds?) to be capped with a greater one, but if so the greater one does not appear in this version. Perhaps a stanza or two is missing. See also the note above on no. XXIII, stanza 7.

XXX. Iorram na Sgiobaireachd

From MacNicol [MN] MS A, folios 5v–7r (=pp.8–11); for other versions see *Checklist*, no.49.

A good few of Murchadh Mòr's songs survive, and there are six of his compositions in the Fernaig manuscript, which also has four by his father, Alasdair mac Mhurchaidh.

In MN MS A and in MacLagan MS 222A the song is entitled 'Iorram na Sgiobaireachd'. Here we can take *iorram* as meaning 'rowing song', for we have reliable evidence that this song was used as such in 1787 (see Ó Baoill, *Eachann Bacach*, p.279). The word *sgiobaireachd* doubtless relates to the fact that in his seafaring exploits the poet (being the leader of a prominent family) would be the skipper (*sgiobair*).

line 3a: from this line the song has been given the title 'An Làir Dhonn' (the brown mare) by John MacKenzie (in his *Sàr-obair nam Bàrd Gaelach*, first published in 1841) and by later editors.

The tune is from S. Fraser, *The airs and melodies peculiar to the Highlands of Scotland and the Isles*, Edinburgh, 1816, no.98, p.48. As given here, there is music for three stanzas, of which the first is the same as the third, but Fraser directs that the first be repeated. Perhaps the song is to be sung with 'rolling' stanzas, as in no. XXVII above.

XXXI. Is Garbh a-nochd an Oidhch' rim' Thaobh

From *Transactions of the Gaelic Society of Inverness*, vol. XLV, pp.178–179, where it was published by the Rev. William Matheson from Dornie manuscript 4, p.19: the manuscript is in the National Library, part of Acc.9711, and was written by Captain Alexander Matheson (d.1897), Dornie (cf. introductory note to no.VI). We have adopted some emendations suggested by Mr Matheson.

The tune used here has not been specifically linked to the present text: it is an adaptation of that recorded in 1954 or 1955 from Miss Annie MacDonald, Lochboisdale, South Uist, an alternative tune for no. XXV, and published in HF, vol. II, p.285.

XXXII. Marbhrainn do Mhac Gille Chaluim Ratharsaidh

From MacLagan [ML] MS 137, pp.26–27; this version is transcribed in *Gairm*, no.145 (1988–89), pp.65–66. We have omitted one difficult couplet. For other versions of the song see *Checklist*, no.289. The vocables given here, however, are not those of ML but those occurring with the tune (see below).

line 8: it seems to have been established now that Iain Garbh did indeed have a brother called Calum, or Gille Caluim, drowned with him on the same occasion (Sorley Maclean, 'Obscure and anonymous Gaelic poetry', *The seventeenth century in the Highlands*, 1986, p.98).

line 9: the Raasay family are a branch of Sìol Torcaill, the MacLeods of Lewis.

The tune given here is a simplified (and arbitrary) transcript from the singing of James Campbell (1897–1979), Kintail, on the disc TNGM 140 (side 2, band 1), for which it was recorded in 1957: see notes on no.XX above. From the point of view of our transcript Mr Campbell's singing seems excessively slow, and *ad libitum*, but it must be remembered that he is the tradition-bearer and that the transcript can only, at best, provide a guide to what he sings. A better transcription appears in Donald A. Fergusson, *From the farthest Hebrides*, Toronto: Macmillan of Canada, 1978, p.265.

XXXIII. Moladh na Pìoba

From Hector Maclean's manuscript of 1738–1768 [HM], now in Halifax, Nova Scotia, p.17; this is the only primary source. The background to the poem is discussed in Derick S. Thomson, 'Niall Mòr MacMhuirich' (1974), TGSI XLIX, pp.19–20.

Because of the strange spelling used in HM, the text given here has been obtained by means of some very speculative and questionable interpretations and emendations of the manuscript text.

line 5d: Hiort, i.e. St Kilda.

line 6c: HM has maodh. Perhaps we should read magh, '(battle)field', instead of modh.

Metrically this poem seems to be based mainly, though loosely, on rannaigheacht mhór (7^1+7^1), but the opening stanza more closely resembles séadna (8^2+7^1).

XXXIV. Biodh an Uidheam seo Triall

From HM pp.96–97, with a few readings from the version in Turner's collection, pp.111–114; the song is edited from four sources in Annie M. Mackenzie, Orain Iain Luim, pp.132–134.

The tune is taken from the Angus Fraser manuscript (Gen.614) in Edinburgh University Library, where it appears harmonised as no.185 on p.88 of one of the rather disorganised sections of the collection. The music there is enough for four stanzas, but what we have given as the first section (for the first of the four stanzas) appears in the manuscript for the first, second and fourth: the manuscript's third section is our second. It seems likely that, whether or not any stanzas are to be repeated, the two sections of the tune would alternate throughout. The heading there is 'Biodh an uigheam So triall. The bard equipped for his Circuit of Visits'.

XXXV. Luinneag Mhic Neachdainn

From Turner's collection (1813), pp.380–383, which appears to be the only source. We have no means of identifying the poet. For some discussion of the meaning of the term luinneag in the title see Scottish Studies 12 (1968), p. 39.

lines 1f-g: the MacNaughton lands around Dùn dà Ràmh are known as 'Leitir Mhic Neachdainn', and Glen Shira was an important part of the family lands.

line 5e: an early-fourteenth-century MacNaughton chief is said to have been a kinsman and 'an assistant of Mac Dugal, Lord of Lorn', whose seat was Dùn Ollaidh near Oban (Angus I. Macnaghten, The chiefs *of Clan Macnachtan*, Windsor: Oxley, 1951, p.19).

line 6a: perhaps the reference here is to Alasdair's brother Iain (Macnaghten, *Clan Macnachtan*, p.35).

line 9c: perhaps a reference to the fact that Alasdair's mother (named in line 13a) was Ealasaid Murray. However, there is an account of the family (though perhaps a semi-learned one of recent origin) which claims that the MacNaughton family were forcibly transplanted from Moray to Perthshire by Malcolm IV in the twelfth century (Macnaghten, *Clan Macnachtan*, pp.10–12).

line 11b: 'Mac Raghnaill' is probably to be taken as an equivalent of *Mac Mhic Raghnaill*, the traditional title of the chief of the MacDonalds of Keppoch.

line 11e: Glendochart was the principal MacNab territory at least as early as the fifteenth century.

line 12c: references to the MacAlasdair family of Loup and the MacDonalds of Largie, both in Kintyre and both on the Stuart side in 1689.

line 12e: Donnchadh Dubh is probably Donnchadh Dubh a' Churraic (c.1550–1631), 7th Campbell of Glenorchy, whose seat was at Am Bealach (Taymouth) in Perthshire. One of his grandsons was Sir Iain (d.1686), 10th of Glenorchy, whose daughter Isabel married Alasdair's son and successor, John (Robert Douglas, *The baronage of Scotland*, Edinburgh, 1798, p.420).

line 13c: this line presumably constitutes strong evidence that Alasdair had two sons, though Macnaghten (*Clan Macnachtan*, pp.35, 45) knows of only one, his successor, John.

XXXVI. Marbhrann Thighearna na Comraich

From Irvine manuscript B, pp.197–198, apparently the only primary source. The collection of the Rev. Alexander Irvine (1772–1824), minister of Little Dunkeld, Perthshire, is in the National Library, now numbered MSS 14877–14881 (see Mackechnie, *Catalogue*, I, pp.337–343). The song is edited from this source by Kenneth D. MacDonald in 'The Mackenzie lairds of Applecross', TGSI LIV (1980), pp.449–450.

line 5a: Cailean Ruadh, first Earl of Seaforth, died in 1633; he appears to have had an exceptionally lavish life-style (see Alexander Mackenzie, *History of the Mackenzies*, Inverness: Mackenzie, 1894, pp.243–244).

line 5b: Sir Coinneach, first MacKenzie of Coul, 'a "man of parts," and in great favour with Charles II.' (Mackenzie, *Mackenzies*, pp.604–605), seems to have died before 1681.

XXXVII. Air dha bhith uair an Dùn Eideann

From the Stewarts' collection [S] of 1804, pp.485–487, where the heading goes on to say that the poet was in Edinburgh attending doctors because of an injury to his leg. We have also made use of a version and notes in Uilleam Mac Mhathain, 'Co-chruinneachadh eile de shaothair nam bàrd Uibhisteach', TGSI XLIX (1976), pp.398–427. For other versions see *Checklist*, no.71.

lines 1g–h: the reference is to Holyrood Abbey, where large-scale works of renovation and enlargement were being carried out between 1684 and 1687 in order to provide king James VII with a Roman Catholic chapel (Charles Rogers, *History of the Chapel Royal of Scotland*, Edinburgh: Grampian Club, 1882, pp.ccxix–ccxliii).

lines 2g–h: an alternative translation might read

> While travelling to the peasants
> who'd make a living with a foot plough.

The tune is taken from the Appendix (p.18) to Keith Norman Macdonald's *Gesto collection*, the only source we have found for a tune for this song. It is given there with piano accompaniment, but we give only the melody: it is there headed 'B'annsa cadal air fraoch'.

XXXVIII. Rìgh na Cruinne ta gun Chrìch

From the Fernaig manuscript, as transcribed in Mac Phàrlain, *Lamhsgrìobhainn Mhic Rath*, pp.56–58.

line 7b: the source reads *No legs lahir mi zhi*; we have inserted *mu* to improve the sense, and the syllable-count.

The metre is a loose form of *rannaigheacht mhór* (7^1+7^1).

XXXIX. Coille Chragaidh

From Hector Maclean's manuscript of 1738–1768, now in Halifax, Nova Scotia, pp.4–6. For other versions see *Checklist*, no.231, and for an account of the battle of Killiecrankie see Charles Sanford Terry, *John Graham of Claverhouse, Viscount of Dundee*, London: Constable, 1905, pp.319–345.

stanza 2: it is not clear who Maighstir Cailean is, but he is either being chided for joining the Williamites or being warned against doing so. One candidate might be the Reverend Colin Campbell of Achnaba (1644–1726), minister of Ardchattan. He had become a minister of the (Episcopalian)

Church of Scotland in Ardchattan and Muckairn in 1667 (TGSI LIII, p.476): that parish belonged to the Presbytery of Lorn, of which he was Clerk and which then also included Mull. But after the Revolution Colin Campbell emerged as a very powerful advocate of Presbyterianism (*ibid.*, p.479). He was also highly regarded as a learned man (line 2b), and some poetry by him, in English and Latin (cf. line 2d), has survived (pp. 482–483).

lines 4g-h: this is a proverb, appearing in Nicolson's collection (Alexander Nicolson, *Gaelic proverbs*, Glasgow: Caledonian Press, 1951, p.254.3, and cf. p.283.1) as *Is geal gach nodha, gu ruig snodhach an fhearna.* – Everything new is white, even to the sap of the alder. The proverb is at least as old as the 11th century, for it appears (*is gel cach núa*) in the tale *Serglige Con Culainn* (edited by Myles Dillon, Dublin Institute for Advanced Studies, 1953, line 720).

stanza 8: Iain mac Ailein is evidently giving credit for bravery to those of Mackay's soldiers who fled at Killiecrankie – perhaps he was aware that many of them were Highlanders.

lines 10c-d: *An Dreòllainn* is a poetic name for Mull, the land of the Macleans, who were led at Killiecrankie by Sir Iain of Duart (c.1670–1716).

lines 10g-h: perhaps a reference to the fact that the first fight in Scotland on behalf of king James occurred in June, 1689, when a Maclean force led by Eachann Maclean of Loch Buidhe encountered a Williamite cavalry force led by Sir Thomas Livingstone (1652–1711) at Cnoc Breac, which was apparently near the Boat of Garten in Strathspey, and killed many of them (Alexander Maclean Sinclair, *Clan Gillean*, pp.220, 263).

stanzas 11-12: the Jacobite army at Killiecrankie included a force of 300 Irishmen under the command of Colonel Alexander Cannon. John Drummond of Balhaldy (*Memoirs of Sir Ewen Cameron of Locheill*, Edinburgh: Abbotsford Club, 1842, p.257) was not as impressed with them as Iain mac Ailein evidently was: when they first arrived to join Dundee's army Drummond called them 'three hundred new-raised, naked, undisciplined Irishmen'. Perhaps lines 11g-h mean that the Irishmen removed the clothing from the bodies of those killed in battle.

The tune is from *The Celtic Monthly*, vol. XIX (1911), p.220, to which it was contributed by Calum Mac Phàrlain (1853–1931): he had noted it down from the singing of John Cameron, a native of Baile Chaolais living in Paisley.

XL. Oran Murtadh Ghlinn Comhann

From the Eigg collection [E] of 1776, pp.241–244, with a few readings from the longer version in MacLagan manuscript 59 [ML], pp.6–11. For other versions see *Checklist*, no. 302. The most recent study of the massacre is Paul Hopkins, *Glencoe and the end of the Highland war*, Edinburgh: Donald, 1986.

line 1g: E has *mhic samhain*, and ML has *Mhic-samhain* with a footnote 'Shamsain' (doubtless the Biblical Samson, who is also named in the ML 232 version). It seems likely that we here have the same *Mac Samhain* who figures in one of Nicolson's *Gaelic proverbs* (1951 edition, no.45.8) as 'a kind of mythical savage': *Aran 'us uibhean tioram culaidh 'mharbhaidh Mhic-Samhain*. An Islay proverb (146.2) refers to creatures called *samhanaich* in similar terms.

The detailed literary history of *Mac Samhain* is unclear, but he seems likely to be the same figure whose name appears as 'Mac Samán' in the late-eleventh-century comic tale *Aislinge Meic Con Glinne* (edited by Kenneth Jackson, Dublin Institute for Advanced Studies, 1990, line 73). The story is set in Cork, but includes a poem introducing a group of eight strange characters who were in Armagh, one of them Mac Samán; see Jackson, *op.cit.*, p.48; *Éigse* XXVI, pp.84, 89; TGSI XXXIV (1935), pp.2–4.

Another one of the 'Armagh eight' was *Mac Rustaing*, who may be the basis for the popular Scottish character *Mac Rùislig* (SGS I, pp.210–211; see Jackson, *loc.cit.*).

line 3h: John Prebble (*Glencoe: the story of the massacre*, Penguin, 1966, p.199) takes this to refer to the army officers who were to carry out the massacre. He envisages the poet, Murchadh MacMhathain, joining them at the table of Mac Iain, the Glencoe chief.

line 5e: this line (like lines 6f-h) might be held to indicate that the poet was a member of the Glencoe family, and that therefore the ascription of the song to Murchadh MacMhathain is to be rejected. Another ascription is to Aonghas mac Alasdair Ruaidh, who may have been a brother of the murdered chief.

line 6b: E has *buanteachd*, but ML begins the line *Choisinn buaidh dhuibh*. Perhaps we should read *buan-teachd*, 'extended access', taking it to refer to the easy access the soldiers had to their victims for a fortnight. However, we emend to *buainteachd*, possibly a noun related to *buain*, 'reaping, harvesting'.

lines 6g-h: the meaning of the words is quite clear, but these lines are open to various interpretations and the translation offered here is more than usually speculative.

line 10c: the reference is doubtless to Eilean Mhunna in Loch Leven, the traditional burial-ground of the Glencoe family.

lines 12b-d: the reference is probably to Alasdair Dubh, the effective chief of Glengarry (though the placenames here indicate also part, at least, of the Keppoch lands). The chiefs of Glengarry and Keppoch were Roman Catholics, which may partly explain why Glengarry was the main target for 'extirpation' identified by Dalrymple, Master of Stair. On the morning of the massacre, as he mustered his soldiers, Campbell of Glenlyon told Mac Iain's son that they were on their way to attack Glengarry. On 30 December, 1691, Alasdair Dubh had announced his conditional decision to sign the oath to William, and this may have been what led Mac Iain to do the same (see Hopkins, *Glencoe*, pp.311, 322, 327, 336): possibly the poet feels that some Jacobites are unjustifiably holding Alasdair Dubh responsible for the massacre.

The tune is based on that printed in *An Deo-Gréine*, vol. VIII (1913), p.119, to which it was contributed by 'M.N.M.' (*i.e.* Malcolm N. Munro, Convener of An Comann's Mod and Music Committee, 1908–1924), who took it from 'Miss A.C. Whyte's Mod Prize Collection of unpublished Music, 1912. The melody was taken down from the singing of a native of Glencoe many years ago.' But here we have radically altered the barring and time of the tune, because the published tune (while it may possibly represent a genuine performance) has rhythm and time which seem to us quite at variance with the rhythmical structure of the verse: we have taken the notes of the printed tune and fitted them, regardless of the printed durations, to the Gaelic text of stanza 1. What seems to be an emended version of the same tune appears in *Coisir a' Mhòid*, vol. 2 (1925), p.21, arranged for four-part choir.

XLI. Oran do Mhac Leòid Dhùn Bheagain

From William Matheson, *The Blind Harper*, SGTS, 1970 [BH], pp.58–72, where there are 28 stanzas edited from all the sources. Here we have selected from the BH text the stanzas which make up the oldest version, that of the NLS manuscript 73.2.2, 'Turner MS XIV' (written by Uilleam MacMhurchaidh in Kintyre around 1750), pp.189–193. Matheson suggests (BH, p.132) that shorter versions like this were more commonly written in the eighteenth century than later: 'there is cause to suspect that in the eighteenth and early nineteenth century there was a certain fear of giving offence, not only to the MacLeods, but also to others who betrayed their trust as chiefs and ruined themselves by behaving in the manner so scathingly described in the verses omitted.' Even so, the fourteen stanzas from MS 73.2.2 seem to us to make an incomplete song, and we have added two further stanzas from BH, stanzas 11 and 16.

line 3b: the reference is to the death of Iain Breac in 1693.

line 5d: the *cèile*, 'partner', is apparently the bag of the pipes (BH, pp.136–137).

line 6a: *i.e.* the piper.

line 8e: these 'counsellors' are probably the two dice used in playing backgammon (BH, p.139).

line 16g: i.e. when Iain Breac died he left the MacLeod holdings undamaged.

The tune used here is the first of three provided in BH, pp.160–161, the source of this one being the Angus Fraser manuscript in Edinburgh University Library.

XLII. Cumha Choire an Easa

From NLS manuscript 14876, folio 36a-b. This manuscript, formerly Acc.4309 in the National Library's collection, was written in 1776 by Dr Donald Smith (1756–1805), who appears to have written it mainly from the soldiers and/or sailors on a transport ship in Halifax, Nova Scotia, in that year (see Mackechnie, *Catalogue*, I, pp.344–347). For some information on Donald Smith, who was a native of Argyllshire, see *Scottish Gaelic Studies*, vol. XIV, Part II (1986), pp.11–12. The writing and spelling are very bad, and we have had to take some readings from the longer version in the Eigg collection (1776), pp.16–20. For other versions see *Checklist*, no.21.

line 2d: a discussion of traditions concerning the feast of the Holy Rood in late September may be found in Raghnall Mac Ille Dhuibh, 'Féill Ròid of the Roaring', *West Highland Free Press*, 11 September, 1987, p.13: that day, which Watson (*Bàrdachd Ghàidhlig*, p.293) names '*Féill Eòin Ròid*, the festival of St. John of the Rood', was 'the beginning of the red-deer rut' (*dàmhair*).

line 10b: as is suggested by Alex. Mackay in *The Celtic Monthly*, vol. I (1893), p.151, it seems not unlikely that the reference here is to Dòmhnall Duabhail MacAidh (1591–1649), Colonel Robert's grand-father, who became the first Lord Reay in 1628. The meaning of his sobriquet has not been established, and a pìobaireachd is named after him *Cumha Dhomhnuill Dhuachal Mhic Aoidh* (Angus Mackay, *A collection of ancient piobaireachd*, Aberdeen: Logan, 1838, p.7).

line 11c: this may refer to composition by An Clàrsair Dall of a tune which survives, in fragmentary form, as the pipe-tune 'Corrienessan's Salute', see BH, p.157.

The tune is from *The Celtic Monthly*, vol. I (1893), p.151; the same tune re-appears in vol. XV (1907), p.135, but in neither case is there any clear indication of its provenance. A different tune, learnt by the Rev. William Matheson in South Uist, is given in Collinson, *Traditional and national music*, p.63, with the direction that it be sung 'in free rhythm according to the natural stress of the words'; the same direction should probably apply to our tune.

XLIII. Do Chlainn Ghill-Eain

From *Co-chruinneacha dhan, orain, &c. &c.*, Inbhirnis: Seumais Friseal, 1821, pp.164–165. The book bears no editor's name, but the editor is identified by Donald Maclean (*Typographia Scoto-Gadelica*, Edinburgh: Grant, 1915, p.178) as 'the Rev. Duncan MacCallum, Arisaig', whom we have failed to identify further. This seems to be the only extant primary source for the song.

The opening line is remarkably negative, and conceivably the song may be a response to an earlier song, perhaps beginning '*Is coma leam fhèin . . .*'.

line 1b: the source has *Sir Lachun* here, and we emend to *Sir Ailein* at the suggestion of Somhairle Mac Gill-eain, *Ris a' Bhruthaich*, Stornoway: Acair, 1985, pp.163–164.

Glossary

The reference is to lines of the poems: the first number given is that of the poem. Where the poem is divided into stanzas (including couplets) the second number is that of the stanza and the letter denotes the line; where there are no stanzas only two numbers appear here, the second being the number of the line.

achainteach 40.13b wanting, having requested
aideachadh 41.6h a (musical) statement
aigeannach 15.14, 36.5d **aigeantach** 35.10a, 37.7a high-spirited, lively
ainmhe 18.16a a blemish
airg-bhratach 9.18c (*see note*) clad in a finely wrought mantle
aistise (= **aiste-se**) 17.9b a style of performance
ait(e) 4.6, 20.7a, 14d pleasant
aithrigh 13.2a, 14.1b, 38.7a repentance
anáir 18.11d (= *onair*) honour
an dèidh's 26.6a, 30.6c, **an dèis** 43.2b after
anmhuin 17.7b (= *fantainn*) waiting
aobhaidh 16.13c cheerful
athais 41.13d reproach

baca 37.3c a peat-bank
bann 3.6b a 'band', *an ornament on clothing*
bannach 41.16g (= *bonnach*) a cake
bànran 25.9 (= *mànran*) amorous discourse
barail 24.4d an equivalent, 39.7a, 41.4b, 4e an opinion
barbaireachd 9.6c (*see note*) barb-work
bàrdail 25.30 poetic, satirical
barradh 15.24, 30.6c sealing, nailing
bàth 34.6a, 38.1d foolish
bearcadach 9.17c (*see note*) free-flowing
beathadh 7.5c (= *beathachadh*) sustaining, feeding
bèin-dearg 27.5b red-skinned
bheilibheid 41.12g velvet
b(h)eith 17.5c, 8a, 18.12c (= *bhith*) being
do bhí 7.5c (= *bha*) was
bhuailfeá 17.6a you would strike

bior 30.9c a spur
birlinn 1.4 a galley, an oar-propelled ship
biùgail 41.13f a bugle
bleidhe 7.3c a goblet
bòd 30.3c a wager (?)
bonn-chluas 33.2d a deaf ear (?)
borran 42.13a moor-grass, silver-weed (*potentilla anserina*)
branach 42.18c having corn-husks
brèine 9.7c rottenness
breitheach 42.16c good for catching
breugas 14.2c (= *breugaidh*) will deceive
brice 9.6b speckledness
briogadh 19.9c pricking, piercing
briuas 17.7c (= *bruthaist*) brose
buainteachd 40.6b (*see note*) reaping
bualadh bhròg 8.21 (*see note*) penalty of being struck with a shoe
buaram 6.1c, *in* b. orm nan . . . , 'Perdition take me if . . .' (?)
buidhich 23.10b become yellow
bùth 19.4b, 23.7b, 41.13e a shop, booth

caitein 35.6f a 'tail', the ribbon hanging at the back of a bonnet
càl 37.4d cabbage; 20.19d cabbage-water
calpa 35.6b calf (of the leg), 9.8c the thickest part of the shaft of an arrow
calpa 26.3c a fixed tax
caoineil 16.12b dry, seasoned
caradh 24.5d (= *càradh*?) fixing, arranging, (= *carachadh*?) moving
cart 16.14c a charter
cas 16.9c (*in passive*) meet
cas-chaibe 41.14f a spade
ceapail 10.2b hitting (a target)
ceilear 30.13c one who hides, a stalker (?)
(do-)chuaidh 18.9a, 20.1c, 32.1d, 2b, 33.3d, 41.6d (= *chaidh*) went
cillein 9.21c a pile, a heap
cladhamhail 18.10d wavy
claigeann 40.13a the 'head' of a rudder
clódh 17.6d changing, overturning
cnapraich 41.8c rattling
cnú 18.1c (= *cnò*) (a) a nut; (b) a loved one
coimeas 17.5b consent, agreement
coinnmhe 7.1b a billeting, quartering
comaidh 17.8a company
comar 42.4b a confluence
comhairleach 41.8e a counsellor (*used of dice*)
còmhdach 39.6f, 39.7b proving, confirming
còmhnardachd 10.15c flatness, smoothness
comhuideacht 18.5d company
connbhaidh 7.4b (= *cumaidh*) keeps, supports

corrach 31.24 loose, unsteady
corrbhinneach 31.22 a tall-sailed vessel
crag 3.23a (= *creag*) a rock
cràighiach 42.16b having shelduck (*tadorna tadorna*)
crann 3.11a, 27.9a an arrow; 3.12a, 33.7a, 40.2f a standard, a banner;
    8.15, 31.9 (?), 40.13c a mast; 16.7a a bolt; 18.9a, 38.5a (the) cross;
    22.5h an antler; 41.14e a plough
créad 17.4b what
criosgheal 31.9 white-belted
cruit 19.19a, 30.7c a harp
cuibhe 11.4d (= *cubhaidh*) proper
cuilm 28.28a a banquet; **cuirm** 7.1c ale
cùl 16.10b, 19.7a the 'backing' (made of vellum) of a bow
cuma 2.11a, 8.12 why
cumha 31.29 a match, something given in exchange
cunbhail 3.13b (= *cumail*) keeping
cungnamh 18.15c (= *còmhnadh*) helping
cupaill 1.23 the shrouds of a ship
cùradh (= *ciùrradh*) 10.1a injuring
cùrsan 24.5c a race (?)

dá 17.4a, 12b, 18.11b if
dàimh 9.14a, 18b, 40.11d a band of poets
dá(i)l 17.13b, 26.10c a condition, a procedure
damadh 18.15a (= *nam bu*) if it were
dán díreach 17.10a strict syllabic verse
deaghadhbhrach 17.1b (*deagh* + *adhbhar-*) of good substance
dearlaig 18.8a bestow, endow
nach dearna 17.9a (= *nach do rinn*) did not do; **go ndearna** 18.9d (=
    gun do rinn) did
deàrna 8.21 palm of the hand
ad dheoidh 17.7a after you; **fa dheòidh** 33.7b in the end
diasfholt 18.10d hair like ears of corn
diùbha 3.20a, **diù** 37.5f an object of contempt
diùchar 39.4e expelling
dlaoi 17.10a shelter
dlùthadh 9.10a, 26.10a fitting closely together
dob 17.4c, 11c (= *bu*) would be
dobrón 17.13b, 18.6a, 14b great sorrow
docracht 17.1d hardship
domhnán 18.5b world
don 8.13 badness (*used in imprecations*)
drillsean 19.21a a lantern
driùchdainn 36.5e dew, tears
druabras 29.10b mud
an dubh-chapall 5.20 *a forfeit* (*see* HF II, *p. 236*)

eàrlaidh 9.14c (= *ullamh*) ready

èidich 10.8b ugly
éidir 17.6d possible
eirthir 8.12 (= *oirthir*) coast
èisg 16.5a a poet
eólchaire 18.3b longing
eugas 27.4b (= *aogas* 36.2h) a countenance, a face

fagháil 18.11c getting
fairgneadh 26.4a (*see note*) hacking; plundering
fàithne 14.4c (= *àithne*) a commandment
falachd 20.11a, **fulachd** 40.4g spite; blood-letting
far 16.13b, 19.1, 43.2c (= *thar*) above, over
far 29.10b, 40.13a (= *bhàrr?*) from, down from
fasadh 41.10e, 11c a stance, an empty house
fàsag 19.16a an empty shell
féad 17.12b, 18.2d (= *faod*) be able
féaghain 18.1d (= *feuchainn*) taking into consideration
fèicheamh 40.12e a creditor (?)
fèile 32.12a a kilt
file 9.19a, **filidh** 5.3 a learned poet
finleach 42.18c having fennel (*fœniculum vulgare*)
fionbhrugh 7.1d (*fíon* + *brugh*) a hall where wine is drunk
fiùbhaidh 16.11a (a) a wooden shaft; (b) an arrow
fiùran 1.24, 19.7c (a) a sapling; (b) a youth
fleasgach 7.3c ornamented with lines or branches
fleòdradh 5.27 soaking, flooding
fògar 39.2f banishing, exile
Fòlaint 39.4f Holland
fós 18.8a, 10a also
fos cionn 38.2b above
frasach 5.16 a manger
fuaghail 3.7a sew, stitch; 15.12, **fuaigh** 30.5b clinch, peg
fuaradh 1.23 the windward side

gàbh 43.4c danger
gàinne 27.10c an arrowhead
gàirdeil 31.7 joyful
garbhcail 9.9c rough, coarse
geig 22.3e (= *ceig*) a clump, a patch of rough weeds
giolla 17.1b (= *gille*) a youth, lad
giort 41.13c a belt
glac 9.5a, 24.6d, 35.2k, 10g a handful (of arrows); 16.12c, 27.8a, 35.2k
    a quiver; 37.7e an embrace
glagraich 37.1h noise, rattling
glùn 23.11b a knee; 17.11a a step in a pedigree, a generation; 20.3a a
    spur (of a hill)
gòirseid 35.6c a gorget, a cuirass
gormleudach 42.17b having green slopes

gràbhailt 19.4a a helmet
greigh 37.4a a herd (of deer)

ibhe 7.1c drinking
iomair 31.10 a ridge between furrows
iomrach 42.14b having ridges
iomthnúdh 18.8b envy
ionnráidh 18.8c noteworthy, worth mentioning
dá n-íosta 17.4a if you were to eat

laoi 7.5a (= *là*) a day
lé 7.5b (= *leatha*) with her, it
dar leanas 17.10d which I have followed
lèidich 6.1b convoying, escorting
ling 5.6, **linnidh** 30.3b (= *linn*) the sea
líon 7.2d a sufficient number
lò 30.15c (= *là*) a day
lòdail 9.11c bulky
lodar 3.20b (= *ladar*) a ladle
lòn 5.15, 37.5h a sheuch, a marsh, a puddle
lònanach 42.14b having little brooks or marshes
lorg 17.10d a track, a path
lughadh 16.10c, 24.12d, 36.2e bending
lùthadh 41.7h a measure, movement (in piping)

màidsearail 34.13a major-like, commanding
marbhach 42.18d given to killings
me 24.1c, 2b, 2d (=*mi*) I
mear 17.3c, 24.5e, 31.8 quick, 18.7a merry
míl 18.7b a warrior, a soldier
mileach 42.13a *some kind of plant*
mìnlachach 42.17b having field camomile (*anthemis nobilis*)
mionn 18.14c a cynosure, object of veneration
modh 17.3c respect; 41.9h *a term in music*
modhair 30.12a (= *modhail?*) gentle
mùgaich 26.10b surliness
munasg 40.9f (= *monasg*) chaff
musgair 9.18b plenty (*?*)

nar 13.2c (= *ar*) our
nar 18.5a (= *nach do*) not
nárbh 18.8c (= *nach bu*) which was not
do neamhlorg 17.7d to fail to seek
nì 19.24b, 30.18b wealth
ní 17.6d, 18.8c (= *cha*) not
níor 17.7a (= *cha do*) not
nìor 21.46 may [I] not
niuas 17.7d news (*?*)

nochar 7.5b (= *cha bu*) was not

oirbhire 18.1d a reproach, a taunt
oireachtas 17.2d (= *eireachdas*) assembly
organ 19.20b, **orghan** 34.7b an organ
orra 23.7b (= *air do*) on your

pailte 28.16b generosity, abundance
pàm 25.25 a goal
pannal 20.21c, 24.10c a group, a company
pèidse 23.12a, 41.12a, 13a a page, a servant boy
pìc 35.2e a pike (*weapon*), 9.4a, 24.6b, 35.10f a bow (*weapon*)
pillean 20.6a, 21.52 a saddle
pinne 39.9g piercing
pòr 41.9h a hole

rath 7.2c prosperity
reath 12.1b (= *ruith* 20.8b) chasing
riachach 42.18c given to flaying
rianadair 41.6a a regulator (*i.e.* the piper)
rícheadh 18.12d Heaven
rímhiadh 17.8b (*rí* + *miadh*) high honour
ríoghbhrugh 7.4c (*rí* + *brugh*) a royal hall
ròibein 22.1h whiskers, beard
rùm 5.26 a (spacious) room; **fo rùm** 10.1c indoors

sad 30.8c the froth of waves
saoi 9.11a, 12a, **saoidh** 30.9a, 40.1g a hero
se 11.2d, 41.6f (= *e*) he
sé 7.1a, 5d (= *sia*) six
sean 7.1d (*see note*), 9.21a experienced, veteran
sean 28.1c (= *sin*) that
seinlíne 17.10b (*sean* + *líne*) an old line
sèisteachd 34.4c melodiousness
seòlta 2.7b handsome; 19.14c set on course
sgalanta 16.12b whistling (*of an arrow in flight*)
sgar 30.6b a seam in a boat's planks
sgàthair 40.10a a coward
sgithean 35.2i (= *sgian*) a knife
sgoth 1.5 a kind of boat
sgràth 41.9b distaste
sgread 40.4g a shriek; grief
sgrid 12.4c last breath
sgròban 39.7h a throat
sgùda 31.20 a ketch
siorradh 21.48 deviation; wounding
slagan 1.8, 1.18 (= *lagan* 37.1c) a hollow
slàn 28.22a a challenge

slàn iomradh 24.2a good health! (*a greeting*)
slat 40.13d a boom (*on a sailing boat*); 41.12c a yard (*length*)
slatag 30.14c a stick, a riding-crop
sligneach 20.7b wry, twisted
slógh 7.4d, 33.7a (= *sluagh*) a host, a company
solta 28.3c vigorous
sonnanach 29.16b a champion
sparradh 19.9b fixing in place; 9.22c attacking
spreigeadh 9.16a inciting (*to produce music*)
spreòd 2.7a a projecting beam
sproc 26.1d, 41.5b dejection
sradag 37.6e a flash (*of gunfire*)
stapall 35.10e a 'staple' or 'stapple', *perhaps an ornate nail or staple on a shield*
subh 18.7c fruit
sùdh 30.6b a seam in a boat's planks
sùgh 19.15c, 40.13b a billow, wave

tagra 18.16a pleading against, charging; **tagradh** 41.6g a (musical) theme
tàileasg 19.19c, 24.8c, 34.3c a backgammon board
taod cluaise 1.22 a rope used in sailing
tarbha 18.15a (= *tairbhe*) profit, benefit
targnach 42.18d given to foretelling
teacht 17.9d, 40.1h, 13f an approach, coming
teann-gheall 8.18 a confident bet
teasdadh 41.8b being lost, failing
teirm 12.8c term, life expectancy
tì 9.17a, 19.22b a point (*in backgammon*); **air tì** 34.11b in support of (?)
tobhairt 13.3b (= *toirt*) giving
tocht 18.5b (= *teacht*) coming
toirt 41.1d value, use
torm 10.10c calling (*at cards*)
t(h)rá 17.3a, 9a, 18.1b indeed
tráth 17.12a, 19.5b, 38.1b a time; 32.10b a day (?); 13.4d, 38.7a early
tràth nòin 16.7c, 34.7c, 41.8b evening
tréidhe 17.11c a quality, a characteristic
trog 11.1c (= *tog*) raise
trup 22.4d, 35.2d a troop of horse-soldiers
tuaileas 29.20a an account, a report; a trace
tuaim 33.4d (*see note*) a tomb (?)
tuasgail 12.4b (= *fuasgail*) release, rescue
tuilg 28.28b pride, ostentation

ùdlaich 22.5h a stag
uiste 15.19 (= *uisge*) water
ùmaid 22.5g (= *ùmaidh*?) a boor, a dolt
uraghall 18.11b, **uirigleadh** 40.4d (= *uirighill*) speech, utterance
urrlamh 18.15d (= *ullamh*) ready

Also available from

Birlinn

Popular Tales *of* the West *Highlands*

J. F. Campbell

John Francis Campbell of Islay's great collection stands today as one of the great memorials to Victorian Scholarship, as well as the greatest treasurehouse of Scottish folktales ever produced.

These stories reveal for the first time the full riches of Gaelic oral culture and its world wide links with other oral traditions. As well as providing the only texts of many of the tales, Campbell's work helped preserve many more by raising the prestige of the story-teller and the tales they told in the community.

Re-issued for the first time by in two volumes by Birlinn, with original Gaelic texts, these books are an essential introduction to the long tradition of Gaelic story-telling.

Volume 1   ISBN 1-874744-15-7

Volume 2   ISBN 1-874744-16-5

The Celtic Placenames *of* Scotland

W. J. Watson

First published in 1926, this remains the greatest source
book ever written on the place names of Scotland. A debt to
Watson is acknowledged by every serious student and it still
remains a bible for everyone interested in Scottish history.
Scotland's place names give an extaordinary insight into its
history through which Watson acts as a guide. In authority
and in range it has never been superceded.

The book starts with a general survey before moving on to
deal with the Celtic names of each area. This is the first
paperback edition.

William J Watson was professor of Celtic at the University
of Edinburgh for over 20 years.

ISBN 1-874744-06-8

More West Highland Tales, Vol. 1
Edited by W.J. Watson, Donald MacLean, H.J. Rose

216 x 138mm   May   580pp   1 874744 22X   £12.99

More West Highland Tales, Vol. 2
Edited by Angus Matheson, J. MacInnes, H.J. Rose, K. Jackson

216 x 138mm   May   398pp   1 874744 238   £12.99

John Francis Campbell

The famous *Popular Tales of the West Highlands* represents only
a small part of the collection which J.F. Campbell had built up.
Much more material of the highest quality was left in
manuscript form on his death. These two volumes, originally
published in 1940 and 1960, represent a continuation of
Campbell's work by some of the Gaelic world's leading scholars.
They uncover much more of a tradition now fragmentary or
destroyed.

The range of these stories is wide - from simple fairy tales to
stories based on Aesop's fables, and from epic legend to a
translation of part of the *Arabian Nights*. All bear witness to one
of the last great oral traditions of Europe.

Each story is presented with a facing page English translation of
the Gaelic original.